LEARNING TOMORROWS

Commentaries on the Future of Education

LEARNING TOMORROWS
Commentaries on the
Future of Education

Edited by

Peter H. Wagschal

PRAEGER PUBLISHERS
Praeger Special Studies

New York • London • Sydney • Toronto

Library of Congress Cataloging in Publication Data

Main entry under title:

Learning tomorrows.

    1. Education--1965-   --Addresses, essays,
lectures. I. Wagschal, Peter H.
LA132.L36   370   78-19763
ISBN 0-03-046716-0

PRAEGER PUBLISHERS, PRAEGER SPECIAL STUDIES
383 Madison Avenue, New York, N.Y. 10017, U.S.A.

Published in the United States of America in 1979
by Praeger Publishers,
A Division of Holt, Rinehart and Winston, CBS, Inc.

9   038   987654321

PREFACE

This collection of essays is a direct result of a conference on the future of education, "Learning Tomorrows," held at the University of Massachusetts at Amherst, April 18-21, 1978. The conference, sponsored by the university's Future Studies program, was a diverse, many-faceted exploration of the possibilities and problems facing American education over the coming decades. Approximately 200 presentations were made during the four days of Learning Tomorrows to a total audience of about 3,000 educators, teachers, and students.

This book is an attempt to capture at least a small portion of that diversity in print. The essays contained here have been deliberately edited in such a manner as to make it clear that they are transcriptions of speeches, not formally prepared papers. It is my hope that they read coherently, but still preserve the flavor of spontaneity that comes only in the spoken word. While no book as brief as this one could possible "cover" all that was raised at so wide-ranging a conference, I have attempted to use those speeches that will accurately reflect the range of issues discussed and the diversity of perspectives presented.

Both the conference and this book constitute ways in which we in the Future Studies program are attempting to "make future possibilities more real for others." While many futurists see their task as one of developing reasonably accurate projections of the most likely futures for American society, we prefer instead to devote ourselves to what we see as a more "empowering" end. We are concerned with helping people to envision a variety of alternatives for their futures—both individually and collectively—so that they might begin to see the future as a matter of choice rather than inevitability. To the extent, then, that these essays encourage the readers to imagine future worlds they might otherwise have not considered and—more importantly—to begin taking action toward making such worlds happen, this book will be achieving what we hoped for it.

While there is no strictly logical sequence to the essays, they are arranged—with the exception of mine at the end—from the most general to the most particular. That is, the earlier essays take up the most general, comprehensive views of the future, and the later ones focus more specifically on particular educational issues and on the more immediate future. This arrangement, again, fits with one of our biases in the Future Studies program: the particulars can only be understood in terms of the wholes of which they are parts.

The number of people who have contributed to the task of making this book possible is truly staggering, but some of them merit special thanks: Betty Swasey for countless hours in preparation for both the conference and in transcribing the speeches; Mario Fantini and Dick Clark for their support throughout; and a very special group of doctoral students who produced a major conference with uncanny skill and flair: Al Peakes, Brett Parent, Bob Kahn, Fran Welson, Jim Masker, David Landesman, Steve Anzalone, and Eddie DeAngelo.

"Learning Tomorrows"—both the conference and this book—seems to me a confirmation of the fact that a variety of futures are possible for American education. The more widespread the debate on crucial educational issues becomes, and the more different perspectives and possibilities it encompasses, the more likely will we be to find a future possibility that is worthy of our commitment. With luck and persistence, perhaps we will even come up with and produce an educational system that is worthy of those most precious resources they are intended to serve—our children.

CONTENTS

LEARNING TOMORROWS

Commentaries on the
Future of Education

R. Buckminster Fuller

1

LEARNING TOMORROWS:
EDUCATION FOR
A CHANGING WORLD

I'm deeply convinced that the subject of Learning Tomorrows contains within it the answer as to whether humanity is going to be able to continue much longer on our planet, for we are going to have to acquire an almost entirely new educational system and do so almost "overnight." We are going to have to learn why humans have been included in the design of an eternally regenerative universe and thereafter swiftly to start fulfilling that cosmic function. I therefore feel an enormous responsibility being allowed to be on your platform to discuss such a subject.

The first thing I think about is Professor Percival Bridgman of Harvard, the natural philosopher who, at the turn of the nineteenth into the twentieth century, said, "How do you suppose it happened that Einstein surprised all the scientists? Why were all the scientists caught off-guard?" Bridgman looked deeply into this matter and concluded that the reason Einstein caught all the scientists off-guard was that Einstein was what Bridgman called "operational"; that is, he paid complete attention to, and interconsidered, all the circumstances surrounding any scientific discovery. He did not isolate the discovery, but paid attention to all the circumstances of its occurrence.

I'm going to suggest a way of thinking about Einstein and his operational way of looking at things. This is not an example that he, Einstein himself, used, but it is my own and has become popularly adopted.

We have a man riding across the country, going due west, on a railroad train. He leans out the window and drops a flaming apple. He has another scientist with him, and the other scientist has a sextant to measure angles and he also has stopwatches. They make observations of the flaming apple's trajectory, which they see flying backwards, that is, to the east, and they measure the angular distances it seems to travel and how much time elapsed at each angle. There are two other scientists standing to the north of the railroad at the time the foregoing event occurs. They have sextants, compasses, and stopwatches. They see the apple come out the window traveling westward, and gradually descending to the track. Using their sextants and stopwatches they make accurate observations of exactly what they see. We have another scientist who is standing on the railroad track far to the west, and he sees the flaming apple go very slowly down toward the earth. We have another man who is standing under the railway trestle while this all occurs, and he makes his scientifically recorded observation. We find that all these observations were faithfully made, and yet they were all different. They tallied what distances and in what directions the various observers were from the flaming object, and through how much of an angle it moved, and at what rate. This brought Einstein into thinking about such variable situations and reports as being relative, not only to one another, but also to all other known cosmic variables. Einstein would observe that the rotation of the Earth affected the event. The Earth, the train, the observers, and the flaming apple were all also zooming around the Sun at 60,000 miles per hour.

It is very important to realize that Einstein not only was a teacher but was also an examiner in the Swiss Patent Office, reviewing patents. At that time, the most prominent products of Switzerland were clocks and watches. If you were reading patent claims of people inventing time-keeping devices, the first thing you would discover is that none of the devices is accurate. They all come out of production differently. In each, the producer tries to provide a little more accuracy. I'm sure this made Einstein think very much about Isaac Newton's assumption of time as being a phenomenon that permeated the entire universe uniformly and simultaneously. Newton's was an instant, omnieverywhere exact universe. This brought Einstein into thinking about relative accuracies and so forth.

I want to give you an example of nonoperational procedures in our own schoolroom experience: the teacher goes to the blackboard and says, "You're going to have your first geometry lesson." And she draws a square, and she tells you that a square is an area bound by a closed line consisting of four equal-length edges and four right angles. All her successive plane geometrical figures are accomplished as areas within "closed lines." As she draws, she says, "A triangle is an area bound by a closed line of three edges and three angles."

In all these plane geometry figures, we are taught to see only the little figures that she is drawing on the board. We look only at the area bound by the closed line. We tend to think about only the geometry on the inside of the line. On the outer side of the line, the teacher is asking you to assume that the blackboard surface extends outward to infinity. Therefore the outer area is to her "undefinable."

But the operational fact is that the blackboard does not go to infinity; it gets to its four edges and goes around to the back. It is a finite object. It is a board. It has length and breadth and thickness. The teacher drew on the surface of a closed system. When she drew a triangle, she divided the total surface of the blackboard into two areas by the closed line. She made two triangles: there is the little one to which she pointed. But all the rest of the blackboard is an area bound by a closed line, having also three edges and three angles. Unscrew your blackboard from the wall. Make your little triangle and then check the remainder of the blackboard's surface, front, edges, and back, and you will find the other complementary big triangle. The fact that it goes around to the back does not alter the fact that it is a continuous surface area bound by a closed line of three angles. We were not taught to look at things that way. The board's edges, when viewed through a lens, are rounded, continuous surfaces. Edges are not terminal conditions. They are short radius turnabout conditions. Moebius' strip has an "inside" of the paper and "outside" of the paper. It is a flattened substance but it does not have two sides divided by its "edge lines."

I say to a young man, "Draw me a triangle on the ground." And he draws it, and I say, "You've drawn four triangles." And he says, "No, I've drawn only one." I have to show him that he has drawn four triangles. "A triangle is an area bound by a closed line with three edges and three angles. You'll agree with me that you've drawn it on the Earth. I'm going to take an Earth 'globe' and make a closed line on it, which we call the equator. It is a circle—a closed line—and it divides the whole Earth into two areas, a southern hemisphere and a northern hemisphere. Let's go all the way to the North Pole and draw a circle around your feet. It divides the total surface of the Earth into two areas, a large southern area and a very small but very real—real because we are standing on it—northern area. Now let's draw a triangle around our feet instead of a circle. Now we've divided the whole Earth's surface into two areas, both of them bound by a closed line with three edges and three angles." And the student said, "You must be wrong. The three corners have outside angles of 300 degrees each for a total of 900 degrees. The sum of the angles of a triangle is always 180 degrees." I said, "Where did you hear that?" He said, "Well, they taught me that in school." I said, "The school is wrong. The angles of a triangle never add to 180 degrees, I've got to prove that to you also.

"We have what is called a 'great circle.' A great circle is a line formed on the surface of a sphere by a plane which goes through the center of the sphere. A great circle is the shortest distance between two points on the surface of a sphere. I'm also going to have to prove that to you." I pick up a 12-inch Earth globe, saying, "I'm going to pick a latitude circle, which is what we call a lesser circle because it doesn't go through the center of the sphere." I point to the latitude circle of 80 degrees north latitude. I take a pair of dividers and put one end of the divider on the North Pole and the other end on the lesser circle of 80 degrees north latitude (see diagram).

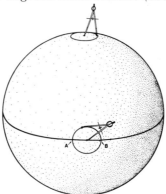

With the dividers fixed at that ten-degree radius opening, I now put one end of the divider on the equator and strike a circle exactly the same size as that of the 80-degree north latitude circle. You now see the equator with the little 80-degree north latitude circle superimposed. With its center on the equator, the little circle crosses the equator at two points, A and B. Quite clearly it is a shorter distance between A and B on the equator than it is on the little circle. I just want to convince you that great circles are always the shortest surface distances between points on a sphere. In spherical trigonometry, we always use great circle arcs for the "lines" connecting points on a sphere.

I am going to look again at our Earth globe (see diagram).

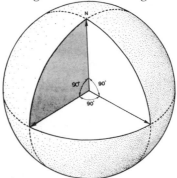

Figures are by R. Buckminster Fuller.

Starting at the North Pole, I take a meridian of longitude, which is a great circle, and go from the North Pole down to the equator. The meridian impinges on the equator at 90 degrees because the equator is produced by a spinning of the Earth around the north-south axis through which the great circle plane of the meridian runs. So, I leave the meridian, turn 90 degrees, and walk eastward on the equator. I changed my course 90 degrees. I now go one-quarter of the way around the Earth at the equator, and take a meridian northward, leaving the equator at 90 degrees. I go back to the North Pole. Because I went one-quarter of the way around the Earth on the equator, the angle of my return to the North Pole is 90 degrees from my starting meridian, so we've got 3 corners each of 90 degrees for a total of 270 degrees, not 180 degrees, as the sum of the angles of a very real triangle, on the surface of the Earth.

Now, see Figure 1.1 and diagram below.

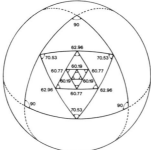

We're going to bisect the edges of that 270-degree triangle, and interconnect the midpoints with great circle arcs to produce a smaller great circle triangle whose corners are 70.5288 degrees each. Bisect that smaller triangle's three great circle arc edges. Interconnect those midpoints with great circle arc lines and get an even smaller triangle, and the three corner angles are 62.9643 degrees each. Bisect that smallest triangle's three arc edges. Interconnect the midpoints and get an even smaller triangle with corner angles of 60.7664 degrees. Bisect its arc edges, interconnect the midpoints, and get corner angles of 60.1933 degrees. With each smaller triangle each corner approaches 60 degrees but never gets to 60; that is, the sum of the angles of an approximately flat triangle is approximately +180 degrees, a limit case which is never reached. The sum of the three angles of all physical triangles always adds up to something other than 180 degrees.

Incidentally, you and I were taught about fractions in school. We were taught how to multiply and divide them, and so forth; we were taught, also, that we couldn't have peanuts divided by elephants. You had to be dealing entirely with peanuts or entirely with elephants. So, when later on we took trigonometry, we were upset when we came to the trigonometric functions, called sines and cosines, tangents and cotangents, etc., and other unfamiliar new words.

FIGURE 1.1

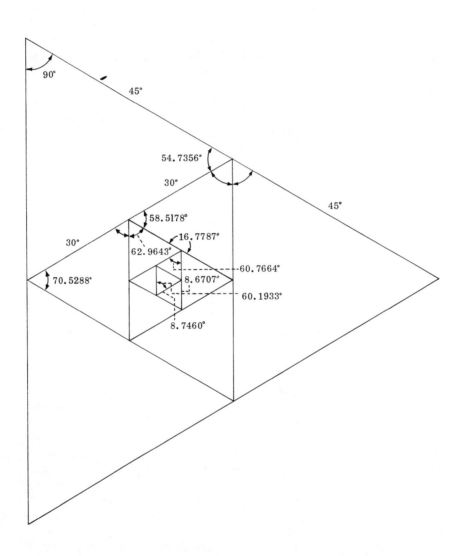

Source: Constructed by R. Buckminster Fuller. Redrawn.

"What is a function?" I asked. The teacher said, "Draw a picture of a right-angled triangle. It has six parts—three angles, A, B, and C, and three lines, a, b, and c (see diagram).

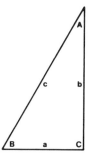

The corner angle C is known because it is a right angle (90 degrees). The trigonometric functions are ratios between any two of the five unknown parts of that right triangle. This means we have ratios between an angle and a line. Ratios are expressed mathematically as fractions. This means we have fractions in which we divide <u>lines</u> by angles or angles by lines." But I had learned that I can't make a fraction out of peanuts and elephants, so how can I have fractions of lines divided by angles?

In order to answer that question, I need to be able to make a drawing on a symmetrical something. A simple way is to draw on a sphere. So let's make a triangle on the surface of an apple, drawn with a knife (see diagram).

With the point of the knife, I draw a great circle-edged triangle on the apple's surface. Then, using the knife's blade, I cut inwardly on each of the edge lines of the triangle to the apple's center, and see that what we call the "edges" or arcs of the triangle are in <u>operational fact</u> the "central angles." We are dividing surface angles by central angles, which is absolutely valid. We are not dividing angles by lines after all.

The fact is that we think spontaneously about omni-dimensional reality, but were taught in school that real life is much too complicated, so they give you their "nice, simple, plane geometry."

They tell you they are starting you with a two-dimensional plane.

Now, I'd like somebody to give me experimental evidence of a surface of <u>nothing</u>. That's where we made the first great operational mistake with that blackboard, by saying it had a surface of nothing, and that the plane went laterally to infinity. There is no infinity. No scientist has ever been there to give demonstrable evidence.

What we should realize is that we're always dealing experientially with something, and all somethings have both insides and outsides. You learn only in reality by starting off with experienceable somethings. If you really are drawing on <u>something</u>, all your lines are measures of central angles.

This is what Bridgman was getting at about Einstein. What are the <u>real</u> physical world circumstances? Don't assume false circumstances where the real circumstances can be found.

The boy to whom I am showing these experiences now agrees with me that, inadvertently, he was wrong about the big triangle as well as the little triangle. He says, "But I didn't mean to make the big triangle." And I say that is the trouble with what humanity is doing today. We've been taught to look at only one side of closed lines. We have a bias—<u>my</u> family, <u>my</u> house, <u>my</u> country. But everything we do is always going to affect not only us, but also all the rest of the Planet Earth <u>and</u> the universe. The very littlest things we do on Earth always greatly affect the total universe.

Then my student says, "You said I had drawn four triangles. You have now proved to me that I've drawn two—a very big one and a very little one—but where are the other two?" I said, "Well, you can only draw <u>on</u> something, and that something always has an inside and an outside." Any something (we'll call all somethings "systems") divides all the universe into four parts: (1) all the universe outside the system, (2) all the universe inside the system, and a little bit of the universe which is the system that does the dividing, which itself subdivides into two parts, i.e., (3) the outward "convex" and (4) the inward "concave." Convex and concave always and only coexist.

When energy as radiation impinges on concave, the latter concentrates the radiation into a beam. When radiation impinges on a convex surface, the radiation is diffused. So convex and concave have completely different physical effects, yet they always and only coexist. I say to the boy, "What you've done is not only to draw the big surface and little surface triangles, but you've divided the whole universe into an insideness and an outsideness. You made, then, a big concave triangle and a little concave triangle, and you made a big convex triangle and a little convex triangle. You made four triangles. You can never make a real universe triangle without making four of them. This is the way everything begins, with four-ness. " This is the four-dimensional world in which we live.

All that I have been explaining is what Professor Percival Bridgman meant by "operational." There was much abstract philo-sophical discussion about "reality" at Harvard, led by Pierce, just before the turn of the nineteenth into the twentieth century, which Pierce called the "school of pragmatism." In contradistinction to Pierce's abstract epistomology, Bridgman wanted a title for a scien-tific grand strategy that was more than pragmatic, and he used the word "operational." This meant dealing comprehensively and in-cisively with scientifically redemonstrable reality and in strictly scientific quantation. The word "operational" has become very much used and misused since that time.

What I've been telling you about, really, is operational mathe-matics. There is always an experiential reality. There is no way you can abstract yourself and take a position outside the universe. You are always in the universe. As integral functions of universe, whatever we do affects the whole universe, every time. We are all complementary parts of universe.

I have one rubber glove, a red rubber glove, and I have it on my left hand. It fits on my left hand beautifully. I'm going to start stripping it off my left hand by rolling the bottom of the cuff of it. As I do, I find it's green on the inside. I keep pulling it, and finally it comes off, and now the red left hand has been annihilated; we have only a right hand and it is green. What we do locally is complemen-tary to the rest of the universe. There's the rest of the universe that fits around my hand, around my body, that is also altered by any and every act. It's always there—that ever, everywhere inter-transforming, nonsimultaneously episoded, eternally regenerative universe.

To comprehend more clearly, we have to electromagnetize our thinking and our communicative vocabulary. What we tune-in and what we don't tune-in doesn't make the non-tuned-in nonexistent. This electromagnetic cerebrating seems to induce a way of thinking about things that is very different from thinking about static space and solid things. We're always dealing with thinkable systems, which are only subdivisions of nonunitarily conceptual scenario uni-verse. A system is a tuned-in episode and not a thing.

I am confident that the way I am talking to you is part of Edu-cation for Tomorrow. Operational comprehensivity and detail are going to spell the difference between whether the world fails to un-derstand what its potentials and realizable options are, and whether we comprehend enough about the functions of humans in universe to be able to employ our mind and exercise our options to establish lasting physical success for all or to perish. We are going to have to learn that it is going to have to be success for all humanity or for none. That goes for an even larger way of thinking, which says it is going to have to be total cosmic success including humanity, or it is going to be cosmic quits.

We must get over the idea of trying to oversimplify education and make it "simple" by making it unreal, isolated, nonoperational. I became convinced as time went on that it is easy to consider myself always as a function of universe, to remove false premises, and to learn that everything I have ever <u>really</u> learned has come from seeing myself in the context of the cosmic working premise. This is the context in which I have been speaking to you.

The next thing I would like to talk about is human beings in the universe right now: how and why we are here. Let us try to understand what all our local problems are, what all problems everywhere are, and what problems have to do with human beings in the universe.

I think that because you and I are so tiny, and our Earth is so big, and the universe is so incredibly incomprehensible we're not thinking very realistically about the rest of that universe.

When I was 28 years of age, Hubble first discovered another galaxy. In the 55 years since that time, we have found a billion such galaxies. We are surrounded by an incredible amount of information, which was not available when I was young, and I want you to think very rapidly with me about our circumstances and our scale. Our Planet Earth is 8,000 miles in diameter. Our highest mountains are approximately five miles above sea level, and our oceans' deepest points about five miles below sea level, so there is a ten-mile differential between the innermost and outermost surface points on our Planet Earth. Ten miles in relation to 8,000 miles is only 1/800th. If I take a 12-inch polished steel ball and breathe on it, the depth of my condensed breathing upon it (1/100th of an inch) is deeper than the ocean on our planet.

I want you to think of us on our real Planet Earth. We have <u>photographs</u> of our Earth taken from space, and you can see the blue of the water and the brown of the land, but you can't make out mountains, or see the depth of the oceans. You can't see any such differential.

Humanity's average height is about five feet. There are about 5,000 feet to a mile, and, as we have observed, ten miles makes the difference between the deepest ocean and the outermost mountain. That difference would be 10,000 of us standing on one another's shoulders, successively one above the other. And since in real universe, looking at our Earth, you can't even see the altitude difference between the mountaintops and the ocean bottoms, you and I are 1/10,000 of invisible on that planet. We are indeed tiny.

We know that our Planet Earth is about 1/100 of the diameter of the sun. You can look at the sun when the thin cloud cover in front of it makes it a white disc. If you take coins out of your pocket and hold them at arm's length trying to cover that disc of the sun, you'll find that a 25-cent piece does just cover it neatly, and that coin is about an inch in diameter. School "rulers" are divided and marked to 1/16 of an inch. Engineers' scales are usually graduated to 1/50 of an inch, but sometimes to 1/100 of an inch. To most human eyes, 1/100 of an inch is a blur. You can't really make out that difference with your eyes. Since our Planet Earth's diameter is only 1/100 that of the Sun, and since the disc we cover the Sun with is only one inch, the Earth as seen against the Sun would be an almost invisible speck of 1/100 of an inch. Our star, Sun, is a mediocre-sized star. One large star, Betelgeuse, has a diameter greater than the orbit of the Earth around the Sun. And our star, Sun, is only one of the hundred billion stars in our galaxy, and we now know of a billion such galaxies. I would say that when we get to that kind of knowledge about our universe, it's clear to me that universe affairs are not dependent upon whether the republicans or democrats are elected, nor is the universe saying we can't afford another galaxy, let alone lunch for the kids. I don't think of the universe as being concerned with the same kind of nonsense that we are. We can develop and hold a bias unreasonably. To me, the universe is something other than just stars to decorate the night.

I'd like to try to be as clear as we can about how and why we are here on this planet. Let's examine what we do know experimentally about ourselves. Let's try to analyze human beings in relation to all other living organisms to see if we can find something different. Yes. All the other living organisms have some built-in, special equipment, part of their physical organisms, that gives them some special advantage in some special environment. There is a little vine that grows beautifully in the Amazon, but nowhere else. I see the birds have wings, so when they're in the sky they can fly. But when they're not flying, they cannot take off their wings, so you see them walking awkwardly, greatly encumbered by their wings.

Human beings are not alone in having brains. Many creatures have brains. Brains are always and only coordinating the information of the senses, taking all the information coming from outside and all the information from our innards. Brains are always and only dealing with special cases—this one smells this way, this one has that temperature—so brains store memories of these special case packages.

But human beings also have a phenomenon, "mind," and human minds have the ability, from time to time, to discover relationships existing between components of a system that are not manifest in any of the components, considered only separately.

Human beings, after millions of years of observing the inverted bowl of stars in the sky, see them as seemingly fixed in rememberable, pattern interrelationships. But against the "bowl" of the fixed star heavens, humans long ago successively discovered five mobile lights a little brighter, bigger, and different in color than the fixed stars. These mobile ones reappeared from time to time, sometimes singly, sometimes in company with one another. Humans in general began to recognize these mobile bright ones, and found there were five of them, which we now call "planets." Humans gave the planets the names of gods, and after a while kept records of their reappearances in relation to the moonths (months), seasons, and years. But humans kept thinking geocentrically, that is, they thought they saw the sun, moon, and stars arising from our flat, fixed world's eastern ocean, all traveling westward through our fixed sky and plunging into our western ocean. Humans needed much more instrumental development and especially mathematical capability to comprehend what was transpiring in a more realistic way: scientific, artifact-proven existence of human mathematical capabilities began only 4,000 years ago in Babylon, when thus first manifest, mathematics were already highly sophisticated. There is a good possibility that our mathematics first developed in the Orient and gradually worked westward through India into Mesopotamia.

Three thousand years ago (that is, a thousand years after the Babylonian mathematics' outcropping) the Greeks made magnificent additions to the geometry and algebra. The Roman Empire monopolized, quashed, and all but obliterated mathematical capability 2,000 years ago. They instituted their Roman numerals as an accounting system which could be employed by utterly illiterate servants. About 1,000 years ago, Arabs and Hindus began relaying ancient mathematical concepts via North Africa into southern Italy and Spain. In 800 A.D. al Kwarazimi first wrote a text in Latin which introduced Arabic numerals into the Romans' Mediterranean world. But not until 1200 A.D. was al Kwarazimi's text published. Because of the general illiteracy of those times, it took 200 years more for the concept of the cyphra (zero) and its function of positioning numbers to reach the students of northern Italy and southern Germany. Positioning of numbers (leftward or rightward) of the successive products of successive integer multipliers, written in successively lower lines, made possible both multiplication and (in reverse patterning) long division. Did you ever try to multiply or divide with Roman numerals? If you did, you found it to be impossible. When I first went to school at the beginning of the twentieth century, the older people of my world, our village pharmacist, butcher, and hardware man, asked in a friendly way whether I had as yet "learned to do my cyphers." That is how the merchants identified mathematics, as a calculating facility to which the cypher was the key.

With the positioning of numbers, Columbus was able to develop navigational competence of a new order. Calculating capability plus telescopic observation made possible Copernicus' discovery that our Earth is a planet going around the Sun with the other planets. Calculation made possible Kepler's, Galileo's, and Newton's further contributions to celestial knowledge.

Mediterranean people began to use Arabic numerals as a shorthand for Roman numerals. The Roman numerals are what we call a scoring system. The masters had a servant stationed at a gate and a herd of sheep being driven through that gate. The master said to the servant, "Every time a sheep goes by, you make a mark." That's how we got our Roman numerals.

The Arabic numerals were probably invented by ancient Arabs to copy the behavior of an abacus. An abacus has a series of vertical rods in a frame. On the rods, beads are mounted in modular groups, five below a horizontal bar and two above for each vertical rod. You enter your progressive products and when you have all of the beads pushed up in the first column, you move one up in the next column. Thus you have a way of accumulating the products, and when you empty the column, and you are trying to keep track of columns in Arabic numerals, you have to have a cypher to indicate an empty column.

Often losing their abacus overboard, or in the caravaning sands, the Phoenicians invented the abak, a tablet sprinkled over with sand on which they drew pictures of the rod and bead abacus array, and on which sand boards they simply entered their single symbols for the number context of the columns. They needed a symbol for an empty column, and invented the cyphra, that is, zero.

Because the Roman world was scoring and could not see or eat "no sheep," they did not comprehend or use the cyphra when they used the other Arabic numerals as shorthand symbols for their Roman numerals.

There came a series of extraordinary new situations and accomplishments now that people could calculate. Not that their intelligence was greater, but they had a facility which had to be developed cooperatively by, and only between, human beings that had been born, all of them naked, helpless, ignorant, driven by hunger, thirst, curiosity, lust, fear, and love, having to find their way by trial and error.

We get to an historical condition wherein calculated informations compound synergetically going back to Copernicus, Tycho Brae,

Kepler, Galileo, and Newton making much better measurements of
the behaviors of those planets, and having calculating capability.
Kepler found that the planets were orbiting the Sun in ellipses and
not in circles. Kepler also found the planets are all different in
size and are operating at different distances from the Sun and are
all going around the Sun at different rates. While they are all on
the same team, they seemed otherwise to be very disorderly.
Kepler, as a mathematician, then said, "I now know one thing about
them: that they are all going around the Sun. If I can know something else that they have in common, then I might be able to find out
other at present unknown characteristics of their planetary system."
In trigonometry, if we have two knowns, we can find out all the other
characteristics of the other unknowns. So Kepler said, "As a mathematician, I'm going to deliberately give them something else in common. I'm going to give them each exactly 21 days of time. This is
much too small a time for them to demonstrate anything except a
rather small arc." So, Kepler assigned 21 days to each, and drew
a diagram of the 21-day behavior for each of the planets. Each one
starts at this known distance from the Sun, and moves in an elliptical
arc, so that at the end of the 21 days the distance from the Sun of
each of the planets is a little bit different from its radial distance at
the start. Each planet's 21-day data described a thin, pie-shaped
form. Kepler then said, "I might as well calculate the areas of
these triangular pieces of pie. There's no pie in the sky, but I
might as well calculate it." I am confident that either you or I
would be mystically overwhelmed if we had been Kepler, making
these calculations and discovering that "the areas swept out by each
of the planets in 21 days (i.e., in exactly 20 days, 23 hours, 59
minutes and 60 seconds) were not just approximately equal areas,
but were exactly the same. It would be quite clear to each of us, as
it was to Kepler, that behind the superficial disorders of experience,
there is some kind of elegantly exact coordinating system. This high
degree of omniinterrelated cosmic coordination challenged Kepler's
intellect. If the planets were touching each other like gears, then he
could understand how they could coordinate. But they are multi-
millions of miles apart. "How can you coordinate celestial bodies at
a million miles apart?" But there were other relevant facts of which
Kepler knew. The first is that the planets were in elliptical orbits.
"If I have a weight on a single restraint string, and swing it around
my head, then its orbit will be a circle," said Kepler. "If I want to
make an ellipse, I have to have two restraints. There's some type
of invisible, cordless tension going on between the planets and the
Sun. When the planets tend to bunch together, they have a more
powerful restraining effect on one another, which brings about an
ellipse."

Human intellect has to imagine, as did Kepler's, the existence of some incredible kinds of tendons that are absolutely invisible; that operate reliably at distances of millions and billions of miles. This conceptioning is an extraordinary challenge to the human mind. We are accustomed to pushing and pulling, but not to that kind of remote control. Kepler knowing that there were enormous weights and enormous size involved to be interrestrained in such an invisible manner, made his stratagems and reasoning an extraordinary human feat.

So then we have Galileo calculating the rate of free-falling bodies, and discovering that the acceleration rate was in terms of the second power of the arithmetical distance travelled.

And then we have Isaac Newton, deeply eager to find out what Kepler's extraordinary cosmic pull might be. Newton was excited by the then popular knowledge that human beings have identified the occurrence of very high tides of the Earth's oceans with the full moon phases. Thinking in terms of this great 6 quintillion tons of ocean lift, Newton realized that when we have a full moon with the Sun on the same side of the Earth as the Moon, the Sun and Moon are both pulling together on the Earth's oceans. The pull would be very great under those circumstances compared to other such times as when Sun and Moon would be on opposite sides of the Earth with the Moon's minor pull canceling some of the Sun's great pull.

Isaac Newton was also greatly advantaged by the astronomers and navigators, who had, by his time, been able to catalog the angular attitudes of the Earth in relation to the Sun and the other planetary bodies for each day, hour, and minute of the year. So Isaac Newton then, using all the foregoing information, hypothesized his first law of motion, which said that "A body persists in a state of rest or in a line of motion except as affected by other bodies." Newton realized that gravitational pull between the Moon, Earth, and Sun must be enormous in order to lift 6 quintillion tons several feet twice daily. He then hypothesized again that the relative initial interattraction of any two bodies in respect to that between any two other equidistanced bodies in universe would be proportional to the product of the masses of the respective pair of bodies. The Earth-Moon-Sun interattractiveness is so great that the pull between two neighboring apples is overwhelmed by the pull of the Earth on both of the apples. Then, Newton thought about the idea of the Earth letting go of the Moon, the way you can let go of a weight on a sling. He then chose a given moment many nights hence when the Moon would be in the full, and from the astronomical data Newton plotted the line of trajectory of the "sling-released Moon" as it departed from Earth as seen against the "fixed" star bowl of the heavens and as seen from a given point on Earth. On that day and moment, Newton observed the behavior of the Moon and "traveled away from that theoretical trajectory and followed the Earth," as the Earth and Moon together went around the Sun at 60,000 miles an hour, while the Moon went around the Earth, and he found the behavior of the Moon exactly verified Galileo's law of "falling bodies." (We shouldn't talk about falling bodies; they are simply being attracted to other dominant bodies.) At any rate, Newton concluded that the interattractiveness of any two bodies was in terms of the second power of the mathematical distance between the bodies. If you double the distance between the two, you reduce the attraction to 1/4 of what it was; if you halve the distance between the two, you increase the attraction four-fold. Newton then made this conclusion his working hypothesis, and the astronomers began to use it. Scientists since then have used it to explain all the celestial behaviors, wherever it could be appropriately employed. We have, then, Isaac Newton's discovery, what we call the gravitational law, mass attraction. If you ask Mr. Newton what "gravity" is, he would say, "There is nothing you can point to." It exists only as the interrelationship existing between bodies. There is nothing in any of the bodies by themselves that predicted they would be attracted to other bodies. It is only because humans for millions of years realized that the planets were, as a team, behaving seemingly differently from the rest of the stellar universe that aroused human curiosity enough to finally discover what was going on between the members of the team that finally disclosed a cosmic law.

I want to point out that this is what human minds have the exclusive capability to discover, namely relationships existing between, that are not in the special cases, whereas the brain is used in apprehending and remembering the special cases.

Newton's discovery is what we call a scientific generalization. To qualify as a scientific generalization means that no exceptions can be found to the operation of the principle, which means that scientific generalizations are inherently eternal. Because it deals only in special cases, all of which begin and end, the brain asks for explanations of how the universe began, and is to end. But the human mind discovered that there is no beginning or ending to eternally regenerative universe. There are only eternal principles.

Human minds have, then, the unique and exclusive capability to discover and express (only mathematically) mind-discovered principles, which are some of the eternal interrelationships (principles) of universe. All of these are synergetic. Synergy means behavior of whole systems unpredicted by the behavior of any of the system components when considered only separately.

As far as we know, only human beings have this generalized principle-discovering capability, and we have now discovered quite a family of these generalized principles. There are not so many of them that we know about, and we never know when we're going to discover one, and we don't know that the last one discovered is going to be the last one at all. But there is an at-present known family, and when we look at them sum-totally together, we learn something very fascinating: none of them has ever been found to contradict any of the others. Not only are they eternal, but they are all interaccommodative. When you and I use the word design in contradistinction to chaos, we mean that an intellect has sorted out and deliberately arranged the patterning of all the components of the experienced composition as visually, aurally, tactilely, or olfactorily apprehended in detail by the brain, but as comprehensively comprehended only by mind and expressible only as eternal interrelationship, only in mathematical terms by mind-special case human mind discovering eternal a priori generalized mind, the intellectual concept of eternal, interaccommodative principles. It seems that the human mind has limited access to the great design of the universe itself.

Human beings must have some very important function to serve in the universe, or we wouldn't be given such a cosmic capability. What we have to think about is the human's function in universe.

I would point out to you that the most common experience of all human minds throughout history is "problems, problems, problems." In fact, if you're good at problem solving, you don't come to a problemless Utopia. You qualify for bigger and bigger problems.

Quite clearly, human beings have the capability to discover principles and to employ them. But humans can't design a generalized principle. For instance, they can't design a generalized lever. It has to be a special case lever, made of such and such a size, and such and such material. You find, then, that human beings have the capability to discover principles and to employ them. For instance, we have the Wright brothers discovering how to make airplanes glide, then how to engine- and propellor-pull them into flight. Long before that, young boys found out how to make paper darts fly across the schoolroom. Their darts were the prototypes for the most advanced delta wing "fighters" of today. Also, long ago, Bernoulli discovered the mathematically stateable law of pressure differentials in gases. Because of Bernoulli's mathematics, humans were able to calculate how to make wingfoils to give us increasing lift advantage in airplanes. And so, today, wingless human beings have made powered wings for themselves, and can fly 42 times faster and 13 times higher than any bird. With their diving equipment, humans can dive deeper and swim faster than a whale. In fact, humans can out-perform all the specially equipped mammals in their special areas of excellence. You can take the wings and fly them, or I can fly them, or we can melt them down and make better ones as they become completely interchangeable between us. Humans have a completely different way of coping with their environment because of their minds' access to some of the principles of universe.

The most important physical fact humans have so far learned about universe is that no energy is being created and no energy is being lost. The universe is eternally regenerative. It is a 100 percent efficient system. In comparison, we humans make reciprocating engines that are 15 percent efficient. We make turbines that are 30 percent efficient; we make jet engines that are 60 to 65 percent efficient; we make what we call fuel cells up to 85 percent efficient. Efficient means how much work we can get out of the energy we invest. But our universe itself is 100 percent efficient. It is the one and only completely efficient system of which we know.

For every turn to play in universe there are six moves to be made within twelve equioptimally economical degrees of freedom, six positive and six negative. If you want to make a wire wheel, you'll find you have to have <u>twelve</u> spokes; you have to have three leftward, three rightward, three backward, and three forward spokes. It takes a minimum of twelve spokes, six positive and six negative, to give you a fixed structure. In every system in our universe that has structural stability, there are a minimum of twelve restraints. Nature always does things in the most economical manner. That is why I say that with every turn to play you have six positive and six negative equally optimally economical alternative moves. Mathematically speaking, and from a topological viewpoint, we find that all the lines in the universe are evenly divisible by the number six. With the 12 degrees of freedom and the incredibly high frequency of event occurrences of all the different omni-intertransforming systems of the universe, the frequency of turns to play is such that you can design anything—a daisy or a galaxy. One takes a little longer than the other, but all of these designs are permitted. Thus we discover our universe to be of such extraordinary complexity that everything is everywhere transforming constantly, yet is sum-totally so intercomplementary, although nonsimultaneously, as to be 100 percent accounted for, no energy being created and none being lost.

We begin to see that we have humans on board our planet to discover principles, and to employ them instrumentally, and to gain information. Just within my lifetime, we have developed such powerful telescopes and such advanced photography that we have discovered a billion galaxies. With the opening of the twentieth century, humanity has entered upon a new kind of reality. Up to the twentieth century, reality was everything we could either see, smell, touch, or hear directly. When I was three years old (I was born in 1895), electrons were discovered. This twentieth century brought humans into electromagnetics. Within electromagnetics, we found that every chemical element has a set of unique electromagnetic frequencies which are not tuneable directly by the human eye, but which can be tuned-in instrumentally by what is called a spectroscope. In this century, humans have developed metallic alloys by, for instance, adding 2 percent of copper to aluminum. The aluminum becomes twice as strong in tension, but doesn't weigh any more.

In our twentieth century, we have developed a vast and ever more exquisitely effective invisible capability. In producing structures, we have evolved ever higher tensile strength with the same weight of material. We now have the ability to communicate almost weightlessly with electromagnetics. We are constantly doing more with ever less investment of physical resources per each magnitude of functional capability.

A new era of human affairs has been opened to us. In 1930, the first chart of the vast electromagnetic spectrum was published (in the United States). All the different chemical elements are present and all the radio wave lengths, the x-rays, infra-reds, and then the red, orange, yellow, green, blue, and violet wave lengths into which you and I have the equipment to tune-in directly. Then we go on into ultra-violet and further nondirect tunability of humans. We discovered that where you and I can tune-in to reality is, in fact, less than 1 millionth of reality. All of the things that are going to affect all of our lives tomorrow are being conducted in realms of electromagnetic spectrum that can only be reached by instrument. So humanity has a very new relationship to universe with its 99 percent invisible reality.

When we begin to think about the educational problems of humanity, we must think in terms of the whole and its intercomplementarity. We're in for a very important new phase of education wherein, as a prelude, during my lifetime, we have gone from 90 percent illiteracy of total humanity to 90 percent literacy. Our little minds, probing the invisible reality, have discovered some very extraordinary principles. Human beings have been employing these principles of the invisible world, and employing them primarily in the realm of weaponry. The cost to realize use of these principles requires vast amounts of money to buy million-dollar tools. Humanity says "We can't afford that." But when national defense says the enemy is going to destroy you if you don't buy these tools, our political leaders say, "All right, we have to cope with the enemy," and we bring in the highest new scientific capability in order to cope. So we have humanity employing these extraordinary principles primarily for what is called national defense. But the national defense employs scientists to discover with what the enemy is going to attack you next, and this brings the most powerfully opposed political systems into escalating the forms of warfare and into exploiting realistically those highest capabilities of man. And then, after people have produced new weaponry, their old weapon becomes obsolete but they still have the production capabilities for it. So they look around the home front for some outlet, and so we have a gradual fallout of ever advancing technology from the military into the home front.

But we're operating politically on our planet according to a view first considered scientifically infallible in 1800 when Thomas Malthus, professor of political economics for East India Company College, for the first time in history had available for his study the total vital statistics from around our closed system spherical planet. The British Empire was the first spherical empire. All the empires before were flat empires, starting with a flat world civilization with its unknown wilderness extending laterally into infinity. If you didn't like the way things were going, you had an infinite number of chances of reaching the right god by prayer, and all would come out fine. But here we have Thomas Malthus in 1800 with all the vital statistics from around the world, and he found quite clearly that humanity is multiplying itself at a geometrical rate and multiplying its life support at an arithmetical rate, wherefor humanity is clearly designed to be a failure. This concept became, then, the model of all economics and social sciences, an inherently inadequate planetary life support.

Each of the great political systems on the planet is saying, "You may not like our system, but we're convinced we have the fairest, most logical, most ingenious method of coping with an inherently inadequate life support." Because there are those who disagree completely on the method of coping, it can only be resolved by trial of arms which political system is fittest to survive. That's why, for the last 30 years, the Soviet Union and the United States have jointly spent over 200 billion dollars a year on how to destroy most expertly, rather than on how to make our world work; all on the basis that there is not enough to go around, so we don't try to use the great principles discovered by science to make the humans' world work. It was this fact, plus the new era capability to do more with the same weight, that made me resolve 50 years ago to try to reverse our priorities, and to use the high technologies only for livingry.

I was an officer-of-the-line in the United States Navy in 1917, during World War I, and I found a great deal of classified information having to do with the invisible world. When, for example, it came into contact with the enemy, he knew the weight of your ship, and its tonnage, armaments, and so forth, but he did not know that your ship and its armaments were made of metals that can do twice as much with the same weight as did his metals. So he was overpowered and sunk. Much of the highly classified information had to do with doing more with the same, or more with less. You don't find anything in books on economics about doing more with less. Now, it occurred to me then (way back in 1917) that if we could continue doing more with less to cope with the enemy, then we might someday be able to do so much with so little that we could take care of everybody peacefully. In 1927, 51 years ago, I committed myself to following through on that; taking the highest production capabilities of humanity and applying them to the homefront. I found, at that time, that the best single family dwelling that you could find weighed 150 tons. And I found that, using the most advanced aircraft technology and design, you could build it weighing three tons. I now have over 200,000 geodesic domes around the world, as constant proof of producing very much more environment-controlling apparatus with ever less amounts of physical weight of input.

We learned long ago that if you double the length of a ship, you have four times as much ship surface and eight times as much volume or payload. I learned that if I double the size of a dome, I have four times as much surface and eight times as much volume, which means that every time I double the size of a dome, I halve the amount of surface through which an interior molecule of atmosphere can gain or lose energy as heat. This is why icebergs melt very, very slowly, but little icecakes melt very, very fast. The smaller they get, the faster they melt. The bigger they get, the more they conserve their energy and the more energy-stable they become.

So now I am able to say informedly and irrefutably that employing only humanity's proven technology and its already mined and recirculating metals, it is clearly demonstrable that within ten years, we can have all humanity living at a higher standard than anyone has heretofore experienced. During this ten-year time, we can phase out forever all further uses of nature's savings account energies—the fossil fuels and atomic energy (nature's cannibal account). We can live entirely on our energy income. But I find that no one is taking that seriously. If you get into the idea that it has to be you or me, and finally you get hold of money, which makes it easier to take care of me, then you get tied up with an enormous amount of investment. The "money" does not go after low-grade ore when there is high-grade ore right next to it. Money always chooses the way that makes the most money, and in the shortest time. After it uses up the fossil fuel, it goes over to the exhaustion of atomic energy. None of the big governments, big religious organizations, and none of the private enterprises is looking seriously at using only our direct daily energy income. The three great power bureaucracies see no way of putting meters between people and the sun. I know that living entirely on our energy income is completely feasible, and I can demonstrate how it can be done, which means that we don't have to cheat all the generations to come of their chances to survive, which means that I now know that the working philosophy of all our major political systems is wrong—it does not have to be "only you or only me." I could not have come to this proven option until the invention of alloys demonstrated our ability to do so much with so little.

On our planet are 4 billion human beings. Possibly a thousand of them know by their own experience that what I am saying is actually true. Ninety-nine percent of humanity doesn't understand science, because science is using mathematics, which have no experimental evidence. Therefore 99 percent of humanity does not understand science, that all science has ever found out is that the universe is the most incredibly reliable technology, that you and I are very much better technology than any of the machinery we have been able to design ourselves. We have the 99 percent who don't understand science, thinking that technology is something new. The 99 percent connect technology only with weapons or machinery that compete for their jobs. They say, "Let's get rid of it."

All of humanity now has the option to "make it" successfully and sustainably, by virtue of our having minds, discovering principles, and being able to employ the principles to do more with less. We have that option, but humanity has been set against itself by thinking that it's against technology.

From a future educational responsibility viewpoint, nothing is more challenging than the question of how we get the 99 percent to understand technology. The universe is technology. How to induce humanity to teach itself that a design revolution is completely different from a political revolution? The latter vengefully pulls the top down. A design revolution would elevate the bottom, and all the others, to sustainable standards of living higher than the top has ever experienced.

I've discovered that nature has a coordinate system that is completely comprehensible. She is completely four-dimensional, absolutely understandable to a child. I have elucidated this coordinate system in a book called Synergetics (1975), which is now in its third printing by Macmillan.

We have in the world of education a great deal of fear. The vast majority of human beings are worried about their jobs. Human beings are convinced by custom that they have to earn a living to get in on the supposedly inadequate life support. We have, then, nature trying very hard to make humans successful, but people self-frustrated by fear.

There has been thus far a complete inability to take advantage of electronics for helping children to educate themselves by, for example, the radio or TV cassette, where they could get their education directly from the world master of any subject such as, for instance, Einstein, instead of listening to someone who doesn't understand Einstein too well. We have our American children, now, latched on to the TV six hours a day. But they are getting nothing but poison. If we could get conceptual understanding of the mathematical coordinate system of nature on TV for those kids, we could help them to understand exactly how nature designs. The children would soon understand that they could exercise our design revolution option to make it on our planet.

Humanity has, by cosmic design wisdom, always been born helpless, naked, ignorant, hungry, thirsty, and curious, and forced to learn only by trial and error that our mind is everything and our muscle is nothing.

We are coming now into our final examinations, to see whether we're really going to qualify. But muscle and brain cunning are as yet in control of human affairs, not mind. If humanity omni-individually resolves to rely upon its mind, humanity could come out of this, and rebloom into a new relationship with our universe wherein nobody ever again would have to prove a right to live, that we have it automatically. The hydrogen atom does not have to earn a living before it is allowed to act like a hydrogen atom. We're about to qualify that way if we come out with mind in control.

If, in our "final exam," mind comes into control, we will exercise our option to be a physical success—all of us. The function of "Education Tomorrow" can only be exercised for about another eight years before we get to where we either have to destroy ourselves or take the option to "make it." The function of the education of tomorrow is to assure that humanity qualifies to continue in the universe.

When I was young, all of humanity was remote from one another, but today, we're all integrated, we all have to act as human occupants on one spaceship planet. It has to be everybody or nobody.

Recently, nature made a drastic evolutionary move in the following way. Amongst mammals, males cover more geography annually than females because females carry the young. Humans have acted that way, I'm sure, from the earliest time. The father was the hunter, the mother was the consolidator. Not only was Dad the hunter, but he also brought home the news. All the kids of all generations had Dad and Mom as the authority about what all the successive generations' Dads and Moms before them had said was safe to eat or do. Dad brought home the news, and told the kids about things in his own esoteric language. They listened to Dad, and, because he was the authority, they emulated his speech. This brought about more and more dialects, which in turn developed into more and more languages.

When I was 32, in May 1927, all the Dads were coming home one afternoon and the kids said, "Dad, come in quickly. Listen to the radio. A man is flying across the Atlantic." And Dad said, "What? Wow!" and he never brought home the news again.

Nobody ever told the kids that Dad was the authority. He was obviously so. But suddenly, in and after 1927, the kids saw Dad and Mom listening to the radio and repeating to their neighbors the radio broadcasters' news. So, quite clearly, without anyone saying so, the man on the radio was an authority greater than Dad. All the broadcasters were selected for the jobs because of the commonality of their pronunciation and because of the magnitude of their vocabulary. Because the radio broadcasters were the new authority, the children began to emulate their pronunciation and vocabulary. This is where their vocabularies came from. At the turn of the century, in my first jobs, all the workmen I worked with had vocabularies of approximately only 100 words, 50 percent profane or obscene. But suddenly, with the radio, came a larger, more accurate, and rich common vocabulary, everywhere around the world.

The speed of sound is 700 miles an hour. The speed of light is 700 million miles an hour, a million times faster than sound. Sound only works in our atmosphere; light and radiation go right on through our universe. What humans get in the way of information visually is approximately a million times what you get by sound. In came the television. When the University of California students at Berkeley had made their first world news as dissidents, that particular group asked me to come and talk to them. The majority of them graduated in 1966. They were born the year the television came into the American home.

Those students said, quite clearly, "I know Dad and Mom 'love me to pieces' and I love them to pieces, but they don't know what's going on. They don't have anything to do with going to the moon, and they don't have anything to do with going to Korea." So Dad and Mom ceased to have any educational responsibility, and the kids said, "We've got to do our own thinking."

I was brought up in an era when my mother and all the teachers said, "Darling, never mind what you think, listen to what we've got to teach you." Nobody is saying that to their kids anymore. The kids suddenly found out that they had to do their own thinking, and they knew that since we could get to the moon we ought to be able to make our world work.

What happened here evolutionarily was similar to the case of the child within the womb. It has to have oxygen, and mother is where the oxygen is. So mother gets it into her lungs, and through her blood and the umbilical cord into the child. When the child is out of the womb, and able to get its own oxygen, we cut the cord.

Humanity is born naked, helpless, and ignorant, and has to learn by mistakes. By billions of errors, humanity has acquired much information, but the significance of the information has been frequently misinterpreted. Until Copernicus, we were the center of the universe. We had an older world making bad explanations. Then, nature suddenly cut the metaphysical cord.

Thus was created a young world in which every successive child was being born in the presence of less misinformation; every child was being born in the presence of more reliable information. Nature said, "Let's cut the 'metabilical' cord and let the young world do its own thinking."

Of course, the first such free-thinking young peoples' idealism is highly exploitable. While the Soviet Union and the United States spend 200 billion dollars a year on getting ready for war, they also jointly spend about 20 billion dollars on psycho-guerilla warfare. This is waged by breaking down the other man's economy before we get to all-out war. Thus, the Soviet Union and the United States both have pushed narcotics on the kids of the other side, and did everything they could to break down the other one's economy. The psycho-guerilla warfare succeeded in exploiting these kids at first, and then the kids discovered that the politicians had them using their heads for battering rams instead of for thinking. Very rapidly, the young developed immunities to all such political exploitation. I find the young world in love with the truth, abhorring any form of hypocrisy and superficial pretense.

I find this young world guarding and cultivating its sensitivity and doing its own thinking, discovering great mystery. They don't need any religious teaching to recognize the incredible mystery present in life. They try to understand what, how, and why the various integrities manifest themselves in the universe.

I find the young people guarding and cultivating the phenomenon love. Love is a very extraordinary phenomenon—very mysterious.

Each child, then, is becoming successively a little less misconditioned, having a better chance to reorganize human affairs.

Nature is trying very hard to make humans successful. If we do make it, we're going to make it by virtue of that young world and its determination to learn the truth and the synergetic intersignificance of all the truths. Once you give the young world a synergetic clue, they will find they can really understand technology and the universe. Then, knowledge is going to proliferate very rapidly.

Because I see that we have the option to make it does not mean that I am optimistic that we will do so; I think it is absolutely touch-and-go as to whether we will win. I think that whether we are going to make it or not, it is really up to each one of us; it is not something we can delegate to the politicians. What kind of world are you really going to have? Are you going to really go along with experimental evidence, or just the way you were taught? Are you going to revert to letting yourself see the sun setting, the sun rising, when you know that the sun is not rising or setting? For 500 years, scientists have failed to do anything in the educational world about coordinating our senses with our knowledge. "Tomorrow's Learning" could easily teach children to see the Earth revolving in respect to the Sun, if you don't start their lives by saying that it is much more practical to say sunset and sunrise. The way we're going to make it is through each one of us being thoughtfully operational about how we communicate what we know.

Seeing much of the young world all around the world, I would say there is a good chance we can make it. Spontaneously thoughtful individual integrity will be able to win, and that is exactly what the world around young individuals is beginning to manifest.

Wilma Scott Heide

2

THE QUEST
FOR HUMANITY
VIA HIGHER EDUCATION

In the academic year 1974-75, I spent some time as an invited guest-in-residence, without portfolio, at Wellesley College in Massachusetts. During the 1975 winter term, a young woman student was physically raped on the Wellesley campus. Though relatively infrequent (about ten reported cases in the past seven years), it was not the first such tragedy. Justifiable outrage was rampant; urgent meetings were held; guidelines for behavior for women at Wellesley were drawn up; an escort system was developed so women wouldn't be "out" alone. Personnel characterized the campus community as "stunned." A suburban campus in an affluent community seems not to be many people's image of a setting for such a violation as rape.

Money earlier budgeted—but not used—to upgrade the campus security was quickly allocated. For the first time, the college administration even accepted and put into operation the idea of including women as part of the security personnel. In fact, the major preoccupations were with security and the behaviors of women, implicitly suggesting that what the women did, or did not do, made the generative and significant difference. Wellesley College sponsored a self-defense class, taught by a man, that has since been integrated into the ongoing physical education program. This, of course, deprived the women of experiencing another woman as capable of self-defense and of teaching its principles and behaviors.

RAPE AND THE WOMEN'S COLLEGE

It would be accurate to state that, except for a few up-front feminists, "the rape"—and rape in general at Wellesley—was perceived as essentially a violent sexual assault, which it also was.

27

It was not perceived as primarily a political act with forced sexual intercourse as part of its manifestation. Several Wellesley people have characterized the Wellesley response (a behavior which itself is reactive not pro-active) as naive . . . and typical. I would agree.

Liva Baker, a Smith College alumna, writing about the Seven (now Six) Sisters colleges, including Wellesley, notes:

> The real problem of the Seven Sisters is that singly and collectively they found themselves consistently faced with the same dilemmas women in the larger society faced, and they chose to solve (sic) them in the same way, demonstrating institutional timidity and humility and becoming severely limited within the obvious societal and academic parameters. Their survival depends on . . . whether they can become truly innovative, can begin to think in terms of lowering the water instead of routinely raising the bridge, in terms of curriculum, faculty, financing, administration: whether they have dreams in their heads, and whether they can discover the means of making them come true.[1]

Wellesley College has dreams that include careerism and serious education of women and much of it by women, but that alone does not a feminist institution make. I agree with Betty Littleton,[2] and many others, that for women's colleges to be valid, they must be or become feminist. To the extent that they are not, they are indeed sexist and androcentric. This has, does, and will perpetuate the rape of women—intellectually, socially, politically, economically, psychologically and spiritually, as well as physically. I would assert that coeducational institutions need, even more strongly, to confront the dilemmas of women and male chauvinists, consequent to patriarchy, with feminist perspectives, values, and commitments if educational validity is envisioned.

I define rape (in the generic sense) as a penetration and violation of the person—her body, her mind, her spirit. Rape is violence; rape is the application of real or implied force and power. In the physical phenomenon of rape, the rapist compels the victim to submit to penile-vaginal sexual intercourse or other related assaults on the person against her will. In educational rape—in the sense of penetration and violation of consciousness, of intellect, of thought processes—it is the near total control of knowledge by and from men that does violence to persons by diminishing women and glorifying men. Just as a feminist consciousness is apparently necessary to understand physical rape as a symptomatic, sexually-expressed but essentially political act of power of men vis-à-vis women, so may feminist analyses be necessary to recognize the intellectual rape of women in institutions that are patriarchal in style, values, curriculum, emulation, philosophies, and consciousness.

I define education as a process of developing one's faculties, as, indeed, the very quest for our humanity in this case, through both formal and informal higher education. The educational, intellectual, and counseling needs of women simply have not been, and cannot be, met without revised curricular and other programs that include the truth and the whole truth about women—our realities and potential—and, indeed, the truth about men. These are current prerequisites to people's successful quest for their humanity. That will require substantial compensatory and reeducation of most faculty, counselors, and administrators. The educational and intellectual needs of men also require this for all men who reject subtle or blatant misogyny as incompatible with true education. By misogyny I mean both overt woman-hating and covert devaluing or omission of women and our experiences. The quest for our humanity through higher education requires a profound reorientation, as I've suggested, to be humanely valid. There is today no university in the sense of universal truths; there are only semi-versities of essentially androcentric thought patterns that are nearly absent from the thoughts and experiences of authentic (that is, self-defined, self-authored) women. Whatever the conscious intent of patriarchal training (as compared to education, as I would define it), the consequent damages to women specifically, and to society generally, largely derive from, generate, and perpetuate the fragile male ego and its accompanying stress.

I want to state up front that I consider the issues not only matters of educational validity but of ethical integrity. I define integrity as a state of being whole, entire, and undiminished. This meaning applies to individuals, areas of knowledge, and institutional practices. It is not the obviously indecent male chauvinists of both sexes to whom I address these thoughts; I consider such to be criminals almost uneducable except by lawsuit and pocketbook education to correct illegal behaviors. It is precisely the apparently decent and caring people whom I know most educators aspire to be, to whom this is addressed.

Sexism represents, I think, the historically first and basic form of human oppression; it has served to sanction the idea of oppression and the division of people into ruler and ruled, dominant and dominated. Racism, classism, ageism, and homophobia are power dynamics that follow this fundamental paradigm, and thus the sanctioning, of the phenomenon of oppression. All its forms are profoundly inhumane and incompatible with education as I have defined it. Feminism both challenges oppression and portends enormous

potential in eliminating it. The issue is not one of relative seriousness or importance of different oppressions, but rather a matter of
acknowledging the original model of dehumanization from which
other manifestations and patterns derived.

As philosophy, as values revolution, as ethical reorientation,
feminism critiques not only obviously "bad" scholarship but areas
of supposed knowledge that lack women's thoughts and experiences,
and thus lack the integrity of wholeness and entirety. This means
much that is generally considered "good" scholarship, "good"
sociology, "good" economics, "good" philosophy or psychology,
"good" political or other science, and "good" theology is simply in-
valid on feminist terms, partly because it ignores or devalues both
women and feminine values. Put otherwise, it is impossible to discover and include the history of women without rediscovering and
reconceptualizing the endeavor of history itself.[3] As a matter of
fact, most that passes for history itself is ahistorical because it
simply ignores, trivializes, or minimizes the past events of the
majority of the populations, women and girls. So, too, with science,
with sociology, with art, and with every other area of human knowledge: ostensible science is not valid if the truth about women is
distorted, minimized, or absent or if that about men is distorted
and exaggerated.

We who are feminists know how to be dispassionate (as we are
repeatedly exhorted to be), to pretend objectivity that is pseudo at
best and distanced from much reality at worst, but we eschew
pseudo-objectivity. Instead, we opt for the honesty of accountability for our subjective involvement in and with our subjects. Things
and automatons are objective; people are subjective entities. We
are responsible for our actions, like our teaching and our ethics.
It is not responsible to pretend that education and educators of all
disciplines are value free, because it is not true.

Prior to a decade or so ago, sex role stereotyping was not
only normal; indeed, it was considered "natural." While feminism
is not yet considered normal, it is indeed very natural. In a healthy
society, the natural is normal. Before addressing the extraordinary
potential of feminism, I want to note how the traditional intellectual
and spiritual penetration of human consciousness represents a rape
that is against our (mostly women's) will as much as any physical
rape and that it occurs by acts of omission and commission. Not
only is much traditional scholarship against our will, it is little informed by the will of women, especially by the will of women and
men who reject the tenets and manifestations of patriarchy. Essentially, women's colleges have been the only likely alternatives, but
even few of those have been administered by women who also articulate changed consciousness and commitments.

Henry Durant, a key founder of Wellesley College, stated at its 1875 founding that the real meaning of higher education for women was "revolt." Most Wellesley College folks were uncomfortable, at best, with my mention of that a century later. At about the same time (1975), writer Nora Ephron (Wellesley '62) referred to her Alma Mater thusly in her book Crazy Salad, "This college is about as meaningful to the educational process in America as a perfume factory is to the national economy."[4] Florynce Kennedy, a black feminist civil rights attorney and phrasemaker, referred to Wellesley College in the spring of 1975 as a "cupcake institution." Harsh assessments, true, and not because Wellesley and most other women's colleges didn't do the job to which they were committed. Quite the contrary, and precisely because they did: provide academic "education" as good (or bad?) as men's colleges; educate women to essential adjustment to and participation in the status quo; seldom identify with or participate as feminists outside or inside the college to challenge and change the status quo, with notable individual exceptions; subtly or blatantly paralyze any will of students, faculty, and administration to translate the ethics of conscience to "real world" political action. The latter is the most serious indictment of most women's colleges. By implicitly and explicitly accepting and emulating patriarchal institutions and values, the capacity of students to develop and express a contrary will of their own was either a coincidental happening in spite of negative sanctions or the absence of positive sanctions, or that capacity was disempowered in order to render women virtually impotent.

Two caveats here may be useful for the reader. It is important that my observations and assessments of most women's colleges, including Wellesley, not be interpreted as "blaming the victims"—women's colleges and the women therein. I have only profound sympathy for both, yet must mourn their rape and disempowerment which could have been and could be prevented if their implicitly feminist foundings had been and would be translated to explicitly feminist ethics, aspirations, education, and values. I use the metaphor of rape because I know most educators to be too decent to countenance that phenomenon when acted out physically. Also, I want the power of the concept of rape to be understood to have intellectual and spiritual manifestations also against the will of their victims. The rest of this essay focuses on two issues: how the potential of self-defined women is frustrated by institutional acts of omission and commission; and how feminist education would make the differences in preventing educational rape and in validating the quest for our humanity via higher education.

SEXISM AND THE ACADEMY

The overt commissions of sex discrimination in academia as evidenced in employment and admission practices are serious violations of women that are well documented elsewhere, and at least technically accessible to the remedies of civil rights laws and executive orders. It is the covert, but institutionalized, practices of academia that I want to address—practices that are often denied to intend, or to result in, oppression of women and which are not yet accessible by legal remedies.

The conceptual and linguistic use of male imagery and language as the ostensibly generic for all people and the presumed norm for all humans is still a central rape of all women by exclusion from consciousness, and is still a central problem in much of academia. This distorts conceptualization of what has been, what is, and what will be included in and about human affairs. Examples are courses, curricular materials, and class discussions that refer variously to: man and his world; mankind; man and his philosophies, his ideas, his problems, his achievements, his government, his art, his literature, his theology, his politics, his family, his children, his socialization, his civilization, his public affairs, his media, his cities, his farms, his works, his wars (and that's pretty accurate), ad nauseum and ad alienation of women and girls on some level of consciousness. "He" and "him" have similar woman-denial effects, and all place females in the category of subsumed, the other, not normal, or simply missing from imagery and consciousness of, in, and about human affairs.

Again and again and again, academic people deny the effects on consciousness of single sex (male) referents, issue disclaimers in writing and speech by suggesting man and he includes woman and she, and often try to trivialize the issues by implying these are "feminist hang-ups." So, any reader who still doubts the effects on consciousness of single sex referents is advised to substitute woman, her world, she and her instead of he for individual when the sex is unspecified or unknown, and to do this in all writing and speech for one year. After all, woman does include man, she does include he, unlike the reverse (and women are the majority). I've suggested this in speeches, meetings, and writings in 48 of the 50 states in the last ten years, and requested feedback on the experiences of people with the courage and sense of adventure to seriously try this experiment. To date, no one who has tried it and reported back to me ever again will suggest the issue of sexism in language is a trivial, irrelevant, and unimportant determinant of consciousness about human beings and our affairs. There are many other examples: seminar (from semen, meaning male seed), seminal principles allegedly meaning basic but actually male only (again from semen). Such words should be used only for phenomena that are for, by, about, and with males only.

Personification via the language is such a powerful method to evoke and include images—or exclude them—that male-only language is an intolerable practice for any academic setting that pretends to a valid quest for our humanity. Even Wellesley College for Women continues to use chairman for the title of department heads and for the position of chairperson of the Board of Trustees. No position or job has a sex. The town of Wellesley has a newspaper called the Townsman. Yet, the same unsophisticated Wellesley folks who were outraged at the physical rape of a student were also annoyed at attempts of others to end the linguistic, intellectual rape of Wellesley College women and Wellesley townswomen by changing the name of the Wellesley newspaper to The Townspeople or something similarly inclusive.

In the spring of 1975, a former Wellesley College faculty member told me, confidentially, that just two years previously she had been denied tenure at that college because she wanted to focus on women's studies. The reason given was that such an interest was not considered "serious scholarship." She is a highly competent scholar in her field who, apparently, could pursue her legitimate interests only where some feminist consciousness exists or she must use euphemistic subject titles. This is tantamount to a black college denying the need or validity of Black Studies or a dental faculty pursuing the study of teeth. Wellesley College is not alone among women's or coed colleges in its reactive and often reactionary and token response to women's studies courses.

A pro-active approach would (long since) have acknowledged the reality that most higher education courses and curricula are, in effect, men's studies, albeit by other names. This results in a profound social illiteracy about women's past, present, and future that amounts to miseducation. Indeed, the illiteracy is so fundamental and serious vis-à-vis women and minorities that I would recommend that an institution that has any degree requirements include women's studies and minorities' studies as requirements for receipt of an educational degree.

Let's look at the instance of Harvard Semi-versity, still considered by some folks to represent the zenith of educational excellence. In 1976 Harvard, which now includes the women's college, Radcliffe, as "his" wife (economic security and convenience and all that, you know), has in the faculty of arts and sciences about half a dozen courses out of 700 that deal explicitly with women's experiences. Only one or two of these do so from a feminist perspective, according to biology professor Ruth Hubbard, one of only 14 women out of the total of 375 tenured faculty at Harvard.[5] So much for the alleged "advantages" to women of marriages of economic convenience. The men and women of such a patriarchal marriage become as one and that one is the man or the male institution in this case; otherwise it would now be called Harvard-Radcliffe or Radcliffe-Harvard. The sheer power and prestige of the Harvard name, when examined and exposed by feminists, represents a devastating rape of women. I am, indeed, suggesting that a wake for Radcliffe College's convenient "marriage" and a moratorium on the mythology about Harvard's "excellence" would be in the national interest.

The following remarkable excerpt from Betty and Ted Roszak's book Masculine/Feminine graphically conveys some consequences of the masculine/feminine dualities that are alive in academia. As you read it, think about the individual and universal consequences of assiduously—and unnaturally—training girls and women for femininity only, and also boys and men for masculinity only (the very existence of superimposed training demonstrates it is not natural).

MASCULINE/FEMININE

He is playing masculine. She is playing feminine.
He is playing masculine because she is playing feminine.
He is playing the kind of man that she thinks the kind of
woman she is playing ought to admire. She is playing
the kind of woman that he thinks the kind of man that he
is playing ought to desire. If he were not playing masculine, he might well be more feminine than she is—
except when she is playing very feminine. If she were
not playing feminine she might well be more masculine
than he is—except when he is playing very masculine.
So he plays harder and she plays softer.
He wants to make sure that she could never be more
masculine than he.
She wants to make sure that he could never be more
feminine than she.
He therefore seeks to destroy the femininity in himself.
She therefore seeks to destroy the masculinity in herself.
She is supposed to admire him for the masculinity in
him that she fears in herself. He is supposed to desire her for the femininity in her that he despises in
himself.
He desires her for her femininity which is his femininity but which he can never lay claim to. She admires
him for his masculinity which is her masculinity but
which she can never lay claim to.

Since he may only love his own femininity in her, he
envies her her femininity. Since she may only love
her own masculinity in him, she envies him his masculinity.
The envy poisons their love.
He, coveting her unattainable femininity decides to
punish her. She, coveting his unattainable masculinity decides to punish him. He denigrates* her femininity which he is supposed to desire and which he really
envies and becomes more aggressively masculine. She
feigns disgust at his masculinity which she is supposed
to admire and which she really envies and becomes more
fastidiously feminine. He is becoming less and less
what he wants to be. She is becoming less and less what
she wants to be. But now he is more manly than ever
and she is more womanly than ever. Her femininity,
growing more dependently supine becomes contemptible.
His masculinity, growing more oppressively domineer-
ing, becomes intolerable. At last she loathes what she
has helped his masculinity to become (and he loathes
what he has helped her femininity to become). So far,
it has all been very symmetrical. But we have left one
thing out. The world belongs to what his masculinity
has become. The reward for what her femininity has
become is only the security which his power can be-
stow upon her. If he were to yield to what her femininity has become, he would be yielding to contemptible
incompetence. If she were to yield to what his masculinity has become she would participate in intolerable
coerciveness. She is stifling under the triviality of her
femininity. The world is groaning under the terrors of
his masculinity.

He is playing masculine. She is playing feminine.
How do we call off the game?[6]

As you may have noticed, feminists have called off the game
in direct and subtle ways. We are doing it in research, in writing,
in assertiveness training for women, in lessons in listening (really)
for men, in non-sexist childrearing for both sexes, in sociology and

---

*Denigrate is itself a racist word; derogate would do nicely.

politics of feeling and touch, in feminist theology, in futurist alternatives, in women's studies and feminist studies curricula, and in
organization.[7] These, and literally thousands of other actions—
national, international, and local organizations, groups, and conferences as well as new lifestyles, legislation, and changed public
policy are significantly intended to prevent the world from not only
groaning but being literally destroyed by the "terrors of his masculinity." A vital part of that imperative is transcending the either/or—
feminine only for women only, masculine only for men only—values
and concepts, the dominance of academia by masculine orientations
and practices and by males, and the devaluing of feminine realities
and potential as well as the devaluing of women ourselves.

Indeed, "misogyny should itself become a central subject of
inquiry rather than continue as a desperate clinging to old, destructive fears and privileges."[8] How ironic that the business of "civilization," such as it is (colonization would be a better word), has been
accomplished, allegedly, mostly by men, though it is mostly women
who have had the literal civilizing effect; traditional sources, to the
contrary, are profound distortions of human history.

> How this came to be, and the process that kept it so,
> may well be the most important question for the self-
> understanding and survival of the human species; but
> the extent to which civilization (sic) has been built on
> the bodies and services of women—unacknowledged,
> unpaid, and unprotected in the main—is a subject ap-
> parently unfit for scholarly decency.[9]

It is the misogyny, not its study, that is indecent and unfit whether
in academia or elsewhere.

The destructive reality and potential of total, or even near
total, apparent male control of human thought, systems of knowledge, belief systems, or educational institutions and processes is
a part of the terror under which the world is groaning. Even most
men who are or seem personally decent and aspire to be humanistic
use male-only language, exclude from or tokenize women in their
projects, ignore the feminist connections and implications and even
the existence of the women's movement for liberation and rights,
exhibit androcentric values and hierarchies, and even abstract ethics
from life to sacrifice people to "truth" that is not even true. Genuine humanism is impossible without feminism as its integral ethos.

The cast of characters who inform every area of human knowledge must not only be women as well as men, but must include
women of minority races (in the United States) as well as the majority race; must include the economically impoverished; the workers

in the vineyards of the home, the factory, the hotels, the laundries, the marketplaces, the hospitals, the churches, the offices, the community, the neighborhood, the public housing, the farms, and the villages. Not only must this wider cast of characters than the affluent, straight, white male, and those so accommodated, inform and educate students and teachers about human affairs and our environments, but responsible academia must be informed and educated about and by the people, the lives, the thoughts, the home life, the art, the music, the humor, the language, the lifestyles, the families, the health, the aspirations, the values, the spirituality, the achievements, the problems, the strengths and the myths about those generally excluded from academia and its often limited insights. Many of the excluded are the genuine educators.

While my own life, thoughts, emotions, and actions take for granted integration with the lives, thoughts, emotions, and actions of women and men of minority races as—and if—we mutually are interested and willing, I realize this is not yet the norm for many people and our institutions, and my writing cannot take for granted either the focus or integration of my life if I don't articulate its content and meaning. Indeed, there are positive values to some self-selected separatism for some purposes for minority people (in the United States) and for women. I am less sanguine about the separatism of white people and of men. Indeed, white people and men have been deprived, in profound ways, by excluding others and even considering non-white people and/or women as "others."

Michelle Russell wrote "An Open Letter to the Academy" that is deeply moving, provocative, and relevant. The letter might come from black women, from Chicana, from Hispanic, from Puerto Rican, from Native American, from Asian American women, and indeed from minority men, and, surely, from those of any race who are economically impoverished. She addresses her remarks to women in the academy, knowing the men may need them even more. Her insights need to be pointedly integrated with, as well as added to, all I've written in this essay. She acknowledges the interdisciplinary possibilities and institutional restructuring potential of women's studies.

However, Ms. Russell writes:

> I would like to widen the discussion to address the responsibility of women's studies.to those outside the academy's walls: the mass of women whose lives will be fundamentally affected by the version of reality developed there, but who, as yet, have no way of directly influencing your direction. [10]

She characterizes the academy as an ivory tower with an intellectual predisposition "to regard anything dead as good and the living as suspect and intrusive."

The academy is a sanctuary that lies in suspension somewhere between the fifteenth and nineteenth centuries, in Ms. Russell's view, with colonization more prevalent than civilization and barbarism triumphing in the guise of progress. She writes:

> And the primary political and cultural role of Western women and the academy has been to rationalize it . . . as a victimized, accomplice population in this process. . . . Your oppression and exploitation have been more cleverly masked than ours, more delicately elaborated. The techniques, refined. You were rewarded in minor ways for docile and active complicity in our dehumanization.

At this point, I raise an unanswerable question: If white women had not been devalued and subjugated, if feminine (humane) values hadn't been devalued and privatized as if for women only, and if white women hadn't been taught to avoid assertiveness and public leadership, would the white man (literally male) have enslaved the black people? Since we cannot relive history, we'll never know, but my response is: "probably not." That does not erase white women's general complicity, but it raises a prior question still relevant to today's racism in academia and society.

Ms. Russell asks the academy and women's studies what and whose stories we will tell.

> The question is this: How will you refuse to let the academy separate the dead from the living, and then, yourselves, declare allegiance to life? As teachers, scholars and students, how available will you make your knowledge to others as tools of their own liberation?

Ms. Russell writes knowingly of those forced outside academia, or who were never in, and for whom pedagogy has become peripatetic. I identify with this as my own experience, especially these last ten years. We must create our own teaching opportunities, for change agents are not welcome as ongoing residents in academia—the processes in which we're engaged don't fit "neatly into 50-minute hours or a disciplinary definition of field of study." We're variously called scholar in residence, visiting lecturer or professor, or occasional guest or consultant, as academic euphemisms for the accurate feminist-at-large, change agent, or revolutionary thinker (who can only be faculty after death, it would appear). "We carry our texts in our heads and on our backs . . . our wit must stick and have the veracity of experience digested, not just books well remembered. We teach in the world. . . . When hard questions are put to us, we cannot say with smugness, 'That is not my field'; we can only say, 'I don't know.'"[11] And let's all find out and share this in and out of academia.

Yes, I identify powerfully with, and as, the peripatetic teacher and administrator to tens and hundreds of thousands, though as a white woman, and vicariously through the Michelle Russells who have taught me about racism. Though others and I have administered to, and with, countless others, codesigned programs and generated changes that have changed or will transform a society and, indeed, the world, still the academy can, and does, have the audacity and myopia to actually question if we can teach and administer. No, we are not technicians, we are not pedantic teachers; we are prophets and visionaries of a future that needn't pass the academy's understanding until years later. Our community, our neighborhoods, our world that we would make our home, is our academy and can be yours. Pierce the veil of the commonplace and embrace us who are feminists and other change agents, and you will embrace your alienated selves and transfuse the very life blood of academia to celebrate the fullness of life. The rhetoric and rationalizations of affluent white patriarchy are simply incompatible with humanity's search for itself via education.

In art, in law, in philosophy, in science, in history, in academia, and elsewhere the ultimate dialectic may be combining the positive and informative dimensions of the feminine and masculine of both sexes, the subjective and relatively objective, the emotional and rational, the micro and macro aspects of knowledge, into the transcendent syntheses of feminism that lead to some gynandrous-like* balance of mind, of emotions, of soul, in humans and in our affairs. Now, that's a vital core of genuine affirmative action to change not only the cast of characters in academia, but also the scripts and the scripting of higher education, that is truly educational as I would define it: a quest for our humanity. This discussion is lengthy, but the process of unbecoming so traditionally

---

*Gynandry and its adjective, gynandrous, are created and used in lieu of androgyny and its adjective, androgynous, to change the sex-related sequence and to portend the overdue ascendency of the female to her natural places.

academic as to be irrelevant and destructive, requires extended covenanting of the feminist ethos in the human interest if we are to become educators. Our fidelity, our commitment, is to truth.

NOTES

1. Liva Baker, I'm Radcliffe, Fly Me: The Seven Sisters and the Failure of Women's Education (New York: Macmillan, 1976).

2. Betty Littleton, "The Special Validity of Women's College," The Chronicle of Higher Education (November 24, 1975).

3. Indeed, for fascinating and provocative history, read historian Linda Gordon, who works on understanding history from the bottom up not the top down. She documents and chronicles the lives of women and others not considered or expected to be powerful but who influenced history anyway. See, for example, Women's Body, Women's Right, a social history of birth control in America (Penguin Books, 1977).

4. Nora Ephron, Crazy Salad: Some Things About Women (New York: Alfred A. Knopf, 1975), p. 36.

5. Ruth Hubbard, "With Will to Choose," Harvard Crimson (Harvard University, Cambridge, Massachusetts), October 19, 1976.

6. Cynthia Merman, "Foreword," in Masculine/Feminine, ed. Betty and Theodore Roszak (New York: Harper Torchbooks, 1979), p. vii and viii.

7. Signs: A Journal of Women in Culture and Society, edited at Barnard College and published by the University of Chicago Press; Carrie Carmichael, Non-Sexist Childraising (Boston: Beacon Press, 1977); Arlie Russell Hochchild, "The Sociology of Feeling and Emotion: Selected Possibilities," in Another Voice: Feminist Perspectives on Social Life and Social Service, eds. Marcia Millman and Rosabeth Moss Kanter (Garden City: Anchor/Doubleday, 1975); Sheila Collins, A Different Heaven and Earth (Valley Forge: Judson Press, 1974); Elise Boulding, The Underside of History: A View of Women Through Time (Boulder, Colorado: Westview, 1976); Joan Roberts, Beyond Intellectual Sexism: A New Woman, A New Reality (New York: David McKay Company, 1976); Adrienne Rich, "Toward a Woman-Centered University," in Women and the Power to Change, ed. Florence Howe (New York: McGraw-Hill, 1975).

8. Rich, "Woman-Centered University," p. 25.

9. Boulding, Underside of History.

10. Michele Russell, "An Open Letter to the Academy," Quest: A Feminist Quarterly 3 (Spring 1977).

11. Ibid.

Ivan Illich

3

LANGUAGE AS A COMMODITY

This conference deals with the future of education. I hope that
in the near future the demand for education will decline. I call education that learning that is derived from contrived teaching offered
by professionals. The less such education there will be, the better
society could be. When I speak of a cut in the manpower, money,
and prestige of education, I do not simply advocate the reduction of
a trend. I speak about the reversal of a vector. The use of political
means to obtain this reversal seems to me as important in the service of learning as it is in the pursuit of justice. I am not suggesting that a lowering of educational expenditures to, let me say, one-
tenth of present cost would automatically bring about either learning
or justice. I only believe that the trimming of educational enterprise
to a fraction of its present intensity is one of the necessary conditions
on which an equal freedom and opportunity to learn depends. Beyond
a certain, socially critical threshold, a society's dependence on education can be taken as that society's measure of social decay. The
level at which learning, and therefore power, in a society are shared
correlates to the way in which needs are shaped and met. The rising
needs for education that we observe in industrial societies reflect,
by this time, a withering of power on the part of people to define and
satisfy their own needs. No doubt, some rights to equal institutional
instruction are a necessary condition for the exercise of the liberty
to learn. But beyond a decisive point—that each society will have to
explore and define in a political process—professional teaching cannot but undermine the social conditions that foster, enhance, and
equalize autonomous learning. Therefore, in our kind of society,
protection against "education" is a much more urgently needed guarantee to enhance the equality of the poor than is the expansion of
rights to educational service.

Oh how I wished that we could pursue our discourse without further mention of "education"; if this oceanic and mystical term could only—during a moratorium—be banned. It is an alchemic, illuminist version of the myth around which Europe was built: the myth that salvation implies the personal services from the clergy of a universal church. But we still live in the age of education, albeit towards its end. The fact that education is tangential to learning, as pastoral service is to salvation in the church, is a point that—in our age—still must be argued. I will do so by highlighting some points that the history of so-called "mother tongue" and the history of education have in common.

But before I do this, let me remind you that education is a Latin term that designates a specifically female activity. "Educatio prolis" designates that imprinting, nurturing, and sheltering that mothers provide for their infants and bitches offer their puppies. "Educatio" in Latin means that shaping of vision, of gait, and of speech that begins from the womb and ceases with detachment from the breast at the time when "in-fantia"—which literally means speechlessness—comes to its end. In classical Latin, men did not "educate." They provided instruction and "decentia" for boys when they were released from dependence on mother. They teach, they provide instruction for a job, and—exceptionally—what the Greeks called "paideia" for the citizen-statesman. The claim of men on female functions is new. It is as new as the idea of childhood. Education that is provided by males who act for the church or the state represents a deep-seated shift in sex roles that, as such, has so far gone generally unobserved. The societal belief that children need "educatio" outside the home and the neighborhood street implies that, somehow, women have become unfit for the job. Ritual rebirth in a period of segregation and imitation is common to many cultures, but it always equips for a special role, in opposition to that played by others. The discovery of the need for education is something radically new. It implies that what women produce in their nurture is always defective: reproduction of citizens can happen only under male supervision in the classroom, where citizens are "hatched." This transfer of educational function from the woman to the teacher is, of course, deeply consistent with the evolution of industrial man: he is dependent on commodities and estranged from autonomous subsistence. In a future that I would find tolerable, this trend toward bureaucratic motherhood would have to be reversed. The most fundamental of these reversals would be needed in the process by which language is learned.

TAUGHT LANGUAGE

Language has become expensive. As language teaching has become a job, a lot of money is spent on the task. Words are one of the two largest categories of marketed values that make up the GNP. Money is spent to decide what shall be said, who shall say it, how, and when, and what kind of people should be reached by the utterance. The higher the cost of each uttered word, the more effort has gone into making it echo. In schools people learn to speak as they should. Money is spent to make the poor speak more like the wealthy, the sick more like the healthy, and the black more like the white. We spend money to improve, correct, enrich, and update the language of kids and that of their teachers. We spend more on the professional jargons that are taught in college, and still more in high schools to give each teenager a smattering of these languages: just enough to make them feel dependent on the psychologist, druggist, or librarian who is fluent in some special kind of English. We first spend money to make people as exclusively monolingual in standard, educated colloquial, and then—usually with little success— we try to teach them a minority dialect or a foreign tongue. Most of what goes on in the name of education is really language instruction, but education is by no means the sole public enterprise in which the ear and the tongue are groomed: administrators and entertainers, admen and newsmen from large interest groups, each fighting for their slice of the language pie. I do not really know how much is spent in the United States to make words.

Energy accounting was almost unthinkable only ten years ago. It has now become an established practice. Today—but really only since a couple of years ago—you can easily look up how many BTUs or other energy units have gone into growing, harvesting, packaging, transporting, and merchandising one edible calorie of bread. The difference is enormous between the bread that is grown and eaten in a village of Greece and the bread sold by the A&P: about 40 times more energy goes into the latter. About 500 times more energy units went into building one cubic foot of St. Catherine's College in Oxford in the 1960s than was needed to build one cubit foot of the Bodleian Library which stands next door, and which I like much more. Information of this kind was available ten years ago, but nobody felt like tabulating it and it made only few people think. Today it's available, and very soon will change people's outlook on the need for fuels. It would now be interesting to know what language accounting would look like. The linguistic analysis of contemporary language is certainly not complete unless, for each group of speakers, we know the amount of money that was spent on the speech of each person. Just as social energy accounts are only approximate and permit—at best—identifying the orders of magnitude within which the relative values are to be found, so language accounting would provide us with data on the relative prevalence of taught language in a population—which would be sufficient for the argument that I would like to make.

The mere per capita expenditure on the language of a group of speakers would, of course, not tell us enough. Taught language comes in a vast range of qualities. The poor, for instance, are much more blared at than the rich, who can buy tutoring and, what is more precious, silence. Each paid word that is addressed to the rich costs, per capita, much more than each word addressed to the poor. Watts are more democratic than words. Yet, even without the more detailed language-economics on which I would like to draw, I can estimate that the dollars spent for fuel imports to the United States pale before those that are now expended on American speech. The language of rich nations is incredibly spongy and absorbs huge investments. Rising expenditures for tax collection, administration, theater, and other forms of costly language have always been a mark of high civilization, especially of urban life. But these fluctuations in expenditures for language (or fuel) were traditionally of a different kind, incomparable with the capitalization of language today. Even today, in poor countries, people still speak to each other, though their language has never been capitalized except, perhaps, among a tiny elite. What is the difference between the everyday speech groups whose language has received—absorbed? resisted? reacted to? suffered? enjoyed?—huge investments and the speech of people whose language has remained outside the market? I want to compare these two worlds of language, but focus my curiosity on just one issue that arises in this context: does the structure of the language itself change with the rate of investment? If so, are these changes such that all languages that absorb funds would show changes that go in the same direction? In my introductory discussion of the subject I will not be able to show convincingly that this is the case. But I do hope that I will give you enough arguments to make both claims appear very probable and to convince you that structurally oriented language economics are worth exploring.

Taught everyday language is without precedent in preindustrial cultures. The current dependence on paid teachers and on models of ordinary speech is just as much a unique characteristic of industrial economics as is our dependence on fossil fuels. Both language and energy have only in our generation been recognized as worldwide needs that—for all people—must be satisfied by planned, programmed intervention. Traditional cultures subsisted on sunshine that was captured mostly through agriculture: the hoe, the ditch, the yoke

were common; large sails or waterwheels were known but rare.
These cultures that lived mostly on the sun subsisted basically on
vernacular language that was absorbed by each group through its
own roots. Just as power was drawn from nature mostly by tools
that increased the skill of fingers and the power of arms and legs,
so language was drawn from the cultural environment through the
encounter with people, each of whom one could smell and touch,
love and hate. Just as fuel was not delivered, the vernacular was
never taught. Taught tongues were rare, like sails and like mills.
In most cultures we know, speech overcame man.

The majority in poor countries, even today, learn to speak
without any paid tutorship; and they learn to speak in a way that in
no way compares with the self-conscious, self-important, colorless
mumbling that, after a long stay in villages of South America and
Southeast Asia, surprised me again during my last visit to American
campuses. For people who cannot hear the difference, I feel only
contempt that I try hard to transform into sorrow for their tone-
deafness. But what else shall I expect from people who are not
brought up on mother's breast but on formula: Nestle if they are
from poor families, and a formula prepared under the nose of Ralph
Nader if they are born among the enlightened rich, or if they are
foundlings whom the elite tutor in its institutions. For people
trained to choose among packaged formulas, mother's breast appears as one more option. In the same way, for people who learned
every language they know from somebody they believe to be their
teacher, untutored vernacular seems just like another less-developed
model among many.

But this is simply not so: language that is exempt from rational
tutorship is a different kind of social phenomenon than language that
is taught. Where untutored language is the predominant marker of a
shared world, a sense of shared power within the group exists, that
cannot be duplicated by language that is delivered. One of the first
ways this difference shows is in a sense of power over language itself—over its acquisition. The poor in nonindustrial countries all
over the world, even today, are polyglot. My friend the goldsmith
of Timbuktu speaks Songhay at home, listens to Banbara on the radio,
devotedly and with some understanding says his prayers five times a
day in Arabic, gets along in two trade languages on the souk, con-
verses in passable French that he has picked up in the army—and
none of those languages was formally taught to him. Communities
in which monolingual people prevail are rare except in three kinds
of settings: in tribal communities that have not really experienced
the late neolithic period, in communities that have experienced certain intense forms of discrimination, and among the citizens of
nation-states that for several generations have enjoyed the benefits

of compulsory schooling. To take it for granted that most people
are monolingual is typical for the members of the middle class.
Admiration for the polyglot unfailingly exposes the social climber.

Throughout history, untutored language was prevalent, but
hardly ever the only kind of language known. Just as, in traditional
cultures, some energy was captured through windmills and canals,
and those who had large boats or those who cornered the right spot
on the brook could use their tool for a net transfer of power to their
own advantage, so some people have always used a taught language
to corner some privilege. But such additional codes remained either
rare and special, or served very narrow purposes. The ordinary
language, the vernacular, but also the trade idiom, the language of
prayer, the craft jargon, and the language of basic accounts, was
learned on the side, as part of everyday life. Of course, Latin or
Sanskrit were sometimes formally taught to the priest; a court language, such as Frankish, Persian, or Turkish, was taught to him
who wanted to become a scribe; neophites were formally initiated
into the language of astronomy, alchemy, or late masonry. And,
of course, the knowledge of such formally taught language raised a
man above others, like the saddle of a horse. Quite frequently, in
fact, the process of formal initiation did not teach a new language
skill, but exempted the initiate from the taboo that forbade others to
use certain words. Male initiation to the languages of the hunt and
of ritual intercourse is probably the most widespread example of
such a ritual of selective language "de-tabuisation." But, no matter
how much or how little language was taught, the taught language rarely rubbed off on vernacular speech. Neither the existence of some
language teaching at all times nor the spread of some language
through professional preachers or comedians weakens my key point:
outside of those societies that we now call "modern European," no
attempt was made to impose on entire populations an everyday language that would be subject to the control of paid teachers or an-
nouncers. Everyday language, until recently, was nowhere the
product of design; it was nowhere paid for and delivered like a commodity. And while every historian who deals with the origin of
nation-states pays attention to commodities, economists generally
overlook language.

THE VERNACULAR AND THE COLLOQUIAL

I want to contrast taught colloquial and vernacular speech:
costly language and that which comes at no cost. I call the first
"taught colloquial" because, as we shall see, "mother tongue" is
fraught with tricky implications. "Everyday language" might do,

but is less precise, and most other terms that I shall occasionally use caricature one of the aspects of tutored language. For the opposite, I use the term "vernacular" because I have nothing better. Vernacular comes from an Indo-Germanic root that implies "rootedness" or "abode." It is a Latin word used in classical times for whatever was homebred, homespun, homegrown, homemade—be it a slave or a child, food or dress, animal, opinion, or joke. The term was picked up by Varro to designate a distinction in language. Varro picked "vernacular" to designate language that is grown on the speaker's own grounds as opposed to that which is planted there by others. Varro was a learned man, the most learned Roman according to the great teacher Quintillian, librarian to Caesar and then to Augustus, with considerable influence on the middle ages. So "vernacular" came into English in just that one, restricted sense in which Varro had adopted it. I would now like to resuscitate some of its old breath. Just now we need a simple, straightforward word to designate the fruit of activities in which people engage when they are not motivated by considerations of exchange, a word that would designate non-market-related activities by which people satisfy everyday needs—needs to which, in the process of satisfying them, they also give concrete shape. "Vernacular" seems a good old word that might be acceptable to many contemporaries for this usage. I know that there are technical words available to designate the satisfaction of those needs that economists do not or cannot measure: "social production" as opposed to "economic production"; the generation of "use-values" or "mere use-values," as opposed to the production of "commodities"; "household economics" as opposed to the economics of the "market." But these terms are all specialized, tainted with some ideological prejudice, and they often limp. We need a simple adjective to designate those values that we want to defend from measurement and manipulation by Chicago boys or socialist commissars, and that adjective ought to be broad enough to fit food and language, childbirth and infant-rearing, without implying a "private" activity or a backward procedure. Such an adjective is not at hand. "Vernacular" might do the job. By speaking about vernacular language I am trying to bring into discussion the existence of a vernacular mode of being and doing that extends to all aspects of life.

Before I can go on in my argument, I will have to clarify one more distinction. When I oppose taught language to the vernacular, I draw a line of demarcation somewhere else than linguists do when they distinguish between the high language of an elite and the dialect spoken in lower classes; somewhere else than another frontier that allows us to distinguish between regional and supraregional language; and, again, somewhere else than the demarcation line between the language of the illiterate and that of the literate. No matter how restricted within geographic boundaries, no matter how distinctive for a social level, no matter how specialized for one sex role or one caste, language can be either vernacular (in the sense in which I use the term) or taught. Elite language, second language, trade language, and local language are nothing new, but for each the taught variety that comes as a commodity is entirely new. I am not speaking now in detail about these varieties of taught language, but I am focusing on taught everyday language, taught colloquial—which usually is taught standard colloquial. In all of recorded history, one among several mutually understandable dialects has tended towards predominance in a given region. This kind of predominant dialect was often accepted as the standard form, that form which was written—and that form which, earlier than others, was taught. This dialect generally predominated because of the prestige of its speakers. Most of the time it did not spread because it was taught; it diffused by a much more complex and subtle process. Midland English became the second, common style in which people born into any English dialect could also speak their own language, just as Bahasa Malayu became the national tongue of Indonesia. Since both those language-diffusions took place in rather modern times, we might suspect that intentional teaching had something to do with the process. For Urdu, which the Moghul soldiery spread over the Indian subcontinent, teaching has hardly anything to do with the sudden spread.

No doubt, the dominant position of elite or standard language varieties everywhere was bolstered by writing, and even more by printing. Printing enormously enhanced the colonizing power of elite language. But to say that, because printing has been invented, elite language is destined to supplant all vernacular varieties is to put the cart before the horse; it's like saying that after the invention of the atom bomb, only superpowers shall be sovereign. In fact, the editing, printing, publishing, and distribution of printed matter incorporated increasingly those technical procedures that favor centralization and the colonization of vernacular forms by the printed standard. But this monopoly of centralized procedures over technical innovations is no argument that printing technique could not increasingly be used to give written expression and new vitality and new literary opportunities to thousands of vernacular forms. The fact that printing was used for the imposition of standard colloquials does not mean that written language will always be a taught form.

Vernacular spreads by practical use; it is learned from people who mean what they say, and who say what they mean to the person for whom what they say is meant. This is not so in taught language. In the case of taught language the key model is not a person that I care for or dislike, but a professional speaker. Taught colloquial is modeled by somebody who does not say what he means, but who recites what others have contrived. Taught colloquial is the language of the announcer who follows the script that an editor was told by a publicist that a committee has decided should be said. Taught language is the dead, impersonal rhetoric of people paid to declaim with phony conviction texts composed by others. People who speak taught language imitate the announcer of news, the actor of gags, the instructor who follows the textbooks, the songster of engineered rhymes, or the ghost-written president. This language is not meant to be used when I say something to your face. The language of media always seeks the appropriate audience-profile that has been chosen by the boss of the program. While the vernacular is engendered in the learner by his presence at the intercourse between people who say something to each other face to face, taught language is learned from speakers whose assigned job is gab.

Of course, language would be totally inhuman if it were totally taught. That is what Humboldt meant when he said that real language is that speech that can only be fostered, never taught like math. Only machines can communicate without any reference to vernacular roots. Their chatter in New York now takes up almost three-quarters of the lines that the telephone company operates under a franchise that guarantees free intercourse to people. This is obvious perversion of a public channel. But even more embarrassing than this abuse of a forum of free speech by robots is the incidence of robot-like stock phrases in the remaining part, during which people address each other. A growing percentage of personal utterances has become predictable, not only in content but also in style. Language is degraded to "communication," as if it were nothing but the human variety of an exchange that also goes on between bees, whales, and computers. No doubt, a vernacular component always survives; all I say is that it withers. The American colloquial has become a composite made up of two kinds of language: a commodity-like, taught uniquack, and an impoverished vernacular that tries to survive. Modern French and German have gone the same way, though with one difference: they have absorbed English terms and turns to the point that certain standard exchanges in French or German that I have overheard in European drugstores and offices have all the formal characteristics of a pidgin.

NEEDS AND COMMODITIES

A resistance that sometimes becomes as strong as a sacred taboo guards the recognition of the difference with which we are dealing here: the difference between capitalized language and

vernaculars that come at no economically measurable cost. It is
the same kind of inhibition that makes it difficult for those who are
brought up within the industrial system to sense the fundamental distinction between nurturing at the breast and feeding by bottle; or the
difference between the pupil and the autodidact; or the difference
between a mile moved on my own and a passenger mile; or the difference between housing as an activity and housing as a commodity—
all things about which I have spoken in the past. While anyone would
probably admit that there is a huge difference in taste, meaning,
and value between a homecooked meal and a TV dinner, the discussion of this difference among people like us can be easily blocked.
The people present at a meeting like this one are all people who are
committed to equal rights, equity, the service of the poor. They
know how many mothers have no milk in their breasts, how many
children in the South Bronx suffer protein deficiencies, how many
Mexicans are crippled by the lack of basic foods. As soon as I
raise the distinction between vernacular values and those that can
be economically measured, and therefore administered, some pro-
tector of the poor will jump up and tell me that I am avoiding the
critical issue by giving importance to niceties. I distinguish between transportation and transit by metabolic power, between vernacular and taught colloquial, between homemade food and packaged
nutrition. Now, are not the distances covered on foot and by wheel,
the terms used in learned and in taught language, and the calories
ingested in the two kinds of food the same? No doubt they are, but
this makes each of the two activities comparable only in a narrow,
nonsocial sense. The difference between the vernacular movement,
word, or food and that which is overwhelmingly a commodity goes
much deeper: the value of the vernacular is to a large measure de-
termined by him who engenders it; the need for the commodity is de-
termined and shaped for the consumer by the producer who defines
its value. What makes the world modern is a replacement of the
vernacular values by commodities, which—to be attractive—must
deny the essential value of the aspect that, in this process, is lost.

People who feel like modern men experience basic needs that
correlate to commodities rather than to vernacular activities. Technologies that fit into this kind of world are those that apply scientific
progress to commodity production rather than to the enlargement of
vernacular competence. The use of writing and printing at the service of the standard colloquial in preference to its use for the expansion of the vernacular reflects this deeply ingrained prejudice.
What makes the work process modern is the increased intensity with
which human activity is managed and planned, and the decreased
significance that those activities can claim for themselves, rather
than for exchange on the market. In his essay "On the Limits to

Satisfaction," William Leiss argues this point. I will incorporate here some of his argument, because later I would like to show how the process he describes has affected language since the rise of Europe as an ideal. Leiss argues that the radical transformation of individual wants in the process of industrialization is the hidden complement of the attempt to dominate nature. This attempt to dominate nature has, since the seventeenth century, progressively shaped and branded every aspect of public pursuits in Western societies. Nature was increasingly interpreted as the source from which a social production process is fed: an enterprise that is undertaken for people rather than by them. "Needs" designated, increasingly, rights to the output of this process rather than claims for the freedom and competence to survive. As the environment (which formerly was called "nature") became ruthlessly exploited as a resource and as a trashcan for those commodities that were being produced for the purpose of satisfying needs, human nature (which today is called human psychology) avenged itself. Man became needy. Today, the individual's feelings about his own needs are first associated with an increasing feeling of impotence: in a commodity-dominated environment, needs can no longer be satisfied without recourse to a store, a market. Each satisfaction that commodity-determined man experiences implies a component of frustrated self-reliance. It also implies an experience of isolation: a sense of disappointment about the persons that are close. The person that I can touch and cherish cannot give me what I need, cannot teach me how to make it, cannot show me how to do without it. Every satisfaction of a commodity-shaped need thus undermines further the experiences of self-reliance and of trust in others that are the warp and woof of any traditional culture. Leiss analyzes what happens when the number and the variety of goods and of services grow, each of which is offered to the individual, each interpreted as a need, and each symbolically constituting a utility: the individual is forced to relearn how to need. His wants crumble into progressively smaller components. His wants lose their subjective coherence. The individual loses the ability to fit his need-fragments into a whole that would be meaningful to him or her. Needs are transformed from drives that orient creative action into disorienting lacks that call for professional service to synthesize demand. In this high-commodity setting, the adequate response to any commodity-determined need ceases to imply the satisfaction of the person. The person is understood as forever "in need" of something. As needs become limitless, people become increasingly needy. Paradoxically, the more time and resources are expended on generating commodities for the supposed satisfaction of needs, the more shallow becomes each individual want, and the more indifferent to the specific form in which it shall be met. Beyond a very low threshold, through the replacement of vernacular forms of subsistence by commodity-shaped needs and the goods or services that fit them, the person becomes increasingly needy, teachable, and frustrated.

This analysis of the correlation between needs, commodities, and satisfaction provides an explanation for the limitless demand that economists and philosophers today tend to postulate, and for which empirical evidence seems not to be lacking. The social commitment to the replacement of vernacular activities by commodities is, in fact, at the core of today's world. On this ground alone, ours is a new kind of world, incomparable to any other. But as long as this trend subsists, ours is also a world in which the increase of supply of those kinds of things that teachers or fuel lines make will correspond to increasing frustration. In a world where "enough" can be said only when nature ceases to function as pit or as trash-can, the human being is oriented not towards satisfaction but towards grudging acquiescence.

Where shall we look for the roots of this inversion of values? For this transformation of human psychology in the pursuit of the domination of nature? To say that the roots for this inversion lie in the "rise of capitalism" would be to take the symptom for the disease. Socialism that enshrines at its core the provision of goods and services to each one according to his or her needs is just as much dependent on the belief that needs correlate to commodities as any of those doctrines that socialists call "capitalist." The root of the inversion is much deeper. It is, of course, of a symbolic, religious nature, and demands an understanding of the past and the future of "education," the issue that has brought us together. If we examine when and how ordinary everyday language became teachable, we might gain some episodic insight into this event.

Nobody has ever proposed to teach the vernacular. That is, at least as I use the term, impossible and silly. But I can follow the idea that the colloquial is somehow teachable down into Carolingian times. It was then that, for the first time in history, it was discovered that there are certain basic needs, needs that are universal to mankind and that cry out for satisfaction in a standard fashion that cannot be met in a vernacular way. The discovery might be best associated with the church reform that took place in the eighth century and in which the Scottish monk Alkuin, living a good part of his life as court philosopher of Charlemagne, played a prominent role. Up to that time, the church had considered its ministers primarily as priests, that is, as persons selected and invested with special powers to meet communitary, public needs. They were needed to preach and to preside at functions. They were public officials analogous to those others through whom the state provided the defense of the commonweal against enemy and famine, or the administration of justice or public order and public works.

To call public servants of this kind "service professionals" would be a double mistake, a silly anachronism. But then, from the eighth century on, the precursor of the service professional began to emerge: church-ministers who catered to the personal needs of parishioners, equipped with a theology that defined and established those needs. Priests slowly turned into pastors. The institutionally defined care of individual, the family, and the community acquires unprecedented prominence. Thus, the bureaucratic provision of services that are postulated as a "natural" need of all members of mankind takes shape long before the industrialization of the production of goods. Thirty-five years ago Lewis Mumford tried to make this point. When I first read his statement that the monastic reform of the ninth century created some of the basic assumptions on which the industrial system is founded, I had many reasons to refuse this insight. In the meantime, though, I found a host of arguments—most of which Mumford seems not even to suspect—for rooting the ideologies of the industrial age in the Carolingian Renaissance. The idea that there is no salvation without personal services from the institutional church is one of these formerly unthinkable discoveries, without which, again, our own age would be unthinkable. No doubt, it took 500 years of medieval theology to elaborate on this concept. Only by the end of the middle ages was the pastoral self-image of the church fully rounded. Only during Vatican Council II, within our own generation, will the same church that served as the prime model in the evolution of secular service organizations align itself explicitly on the image of its imitators. But what counts here, the concept that the clergy can define its own services as needs of human nature and make this service commodity into a necessity that cannot be foregone by any single human being without jeopardy of eternal life—this concept is of medieval origin. It is the foundation without which the contemporary service or welfare state would not be conceivable. Surprisingly little research has been done on the religious lore-concepts that distinguish the industrial age fundamentally from all other societies. The decline of the vernacular conception of Christian life in favor of one organized around pastoral care is a complex and drawn-out process that I mention here only because it constitutes a necessary background for the understanding of a similar shift in the understanding of language.

FROM THE VERNACULAR TO UNIQUACK

Three stages can be distinguished in the evolution of the vernacular into industrial uniquack—a term that James Reston first used when Univac was the only commercial computer. The first step is the appearance of the term "mother tongue," and monkish tutorship over vernacular speech. The second is the transformation of mother tongue into national language under the auspices of grammarians. The third is the replacement of schooled and educated standard language based on written texts by our contemporary, medium-fed, high-cost idiom.

The "Mother Tongue"

The terms and the concepts of mother tongue and mother country were both unknown until the high middle ages. The only classical people who conceived of their land as related to "mother" were the early Cretans—memories of a matriarchal order still lingered in their culture. When Europe took shape as a political reality and as an idea, people spoke "people's language," the "sermo vulgaris." "Duits" (formed from "theo-disc," a term related to the English "diet") means precisely that. In patriarchally minded Roman law, a person's vernacular was presumed to be his or her "patrius sermo"—the speech of the male head of the household. Each "sermo" or speech was also perceived as a language. Neither the early Greeks, nor people in the early middle ages, made our distinction between mutually understandable "dialects" and distinct "languages," a distinction that people on the grassroot level of India equally do not yet make. During the last three decades I have had the opportunity to observe many hundreds of highly motivated and intelligent foreign academics seeking entrance to village life in South America and then in Southeast Asia. Again and again I was struck by the difficulty these people have, even when they are trained as social scientists, in understanding the lucid simplicity with which people can identify with one—or with several—forms of vernacular in a way in which only the exceptional poet can live a taught language with every one of his fibers. The vernacular was, in this sense, unproblematic up until the eleventh century. At that moment, quite suddenly, the term "mother tongue" appears. It appears in the sermons of several monks from the Abbey of Gorz and marks the first attempt to make the choice of vernacular into a moral issue. The mother-Abbey of Gorz, in Lorraine, not far from Verdun, had been founded in the eighth century by Benedictines, over a church dedicated to St. Gorgonius. During the ninth century the monastery decayed in a scandalous way. Three generations later, by the tenth century, the Abbey became the center of Germanic monastic reform, a parallel, east of the Rhine, of the Cistercian reform-Abbey of Cluny. Within two generations, 160 daughter-abbeys, founded (or engendered) by Gorz were scattered all through the Germanic territory of the Holy Roman Empire. Gorz itself was located near the dividing line between Romance and Frankish vernaculars, and the monks from Gorz wanted to stop the challenge or advance of the competing monks from Cluny. They made language into an issue and a tool for their claim.

The monks of Gorz launched into language politics by attaching to the term "language" a curious epithet, namely, "mother"— an epithet that was ideologically charged at that time in a manner that is, again, difficult for us to grasp. The symbolic maternity of the church, the universal maternity of the Virgin Mary, was central to the experience of personal life and of cosmic reality with an intensity that you can glean only by reading the original poetry of the time or by sitting quietly in front of one after another of the great statues representing either in Romanic art. By coining the term "mother tongue" the monks of Gorz elevated the unwritten vulgate, vernacular theodisc into something that could be honored, cherished, defended against defilement, and otherwise treated like mother should be. Language was consecrated through its relation with maternity and, at the same time, maternity was alienated by one more step into a principle over which the male clergy could claim power. Mother was now honored and managed, cherished and used, protected in her purity and forged into a weapon, guarded against defilement and used as a shield. The professional pastorate, which today we would understand as a service profession, had made an important step in acquiring responsibilities in the performance of maternal functions.

From the Frankish of the eleventh century the term was translated into low Latin as materna lingua, and thus spread throughout Europe, only to be rediscovered and retranslated into various forms of the vulgate in the early fifteenth century. With the concept of "mother tongue," of a supraregional colloquial with highly charged emotional value and a broad audience, a condition was created that called for the invention of moveable type and of print. Gutenberg made his invention when the language that he needed for its acceptance was ripe.

The Grammarian and the "National Language"

The next stop in the mutation of the vernacular coincides with the development of a device by which the teaching of mother tongue could be taken over by men. The medieval preachers, poets, and bible translators had only tried to consecrate, elevate, and endow with the nimbus of mystical maternity that language that they heard among the people. Now a new breed of secular clerics, formed by humanism, consciously used the vulgar as raw material for an engineering enterprise. The manual of specifications for correct sentences in the vernacular makes its appearance.

The publication of the first grammar in any modern European language was a solemn event, in late 1492. That year the Moor was driven from Granada, the Jews were expelled from Toledo, and the return of Columbus from his first voyage was expected any day. That year, Don Elio Antonio de Nebrija dedicated the first edition of his Grammatica Castellana to his queen, Isabela la Catolica. At the age of 19, Nebrija had gone to Italy, where Latin had least decayed and was best cultivated, to bring back to life in Spain the one language that as a young man he had considered worthy and that, in his opinion, had died in barbarian neglect in his home country. Hernan Nunnez, a contemporary, compared him to Orpheus bringing back Euridice. For almost a generation he was in Salamanca, at the center of renewal of classical grammar and rhetoric. Now, in his fifty-second year, he finished his grammar of the spoken language and, shortly afterwards, the first dictionary that already contains a term born overseas: "canoa—canoe," which Columbus had in the meantime brought back with the first sample Indian.

As I said, Nebrija dedicated his grammar to Isabela, who was a very uncommon woman too. In battle she dressed as a knight, and at court she surrounded herself with humanists who consistently treated her as an equal. Six months earlier, Nebrija had sent a draft of the book to the queen. For this draft she had expressed her gratitude and admiration for the author who had done for Castillan what, so far, had been done only for the languages of Rome and Greece. But with her appreciation she also expressed her perplexity. She was unable to understand to what use such a grammar could be put. Grammar was a teaching tool—and the vernacular was not something anybody could ever be taught. In her kingdoms, the queen insisted, every subject was destined by nature for a perfect dominion over his tongue. This royal sentence expresses a majestic principle of political linguistics. In the meantime, this sense of vernacular sovereignty has been largely administered away.

In the introduction to the first edition, which was published in late 1492, Nebrija defends his undertaking by answering the queen. I have translated parts of his three-page argument, because any paraphrase would water it down:

My illustrious Queen. Whenever I ponder over the tokens of the past that writing has preserved for us, I return to the same conclusion: Language has forever been the mate of empire and always shall

remain its comrade. Together they start, together
they grow and flower, together they decline.

Please notice the shift from "mother" to "mate." Please notice the
new betrothal of "armas y letras"—the military and the university.
Please notice how the ever changing patterns of vernacular speech
may now be held up against a standard language that measures their
improvement and their debasement.

> Castillan went through its infancy at the time of the
> judges . . . it waxed in strength under Alphonse the
> Wise who gathered laws and histories and who had
> many Arabic and Latin works translated.

Indeed, Alphonse X was the first European monarch who used his
native tongue to insist that he was no longer a Latin king. His translators were mostly Jews, who preferred the vulgar tongue over the
Church's Latin. Please notice Nebrija's awareness that the standard
language is strengthened as it is used for the writing of history, as
a medium for translation and for the embodiment of laws.

> Thus our language followed our soldiers whom we sent
> abroad to rule. It spread to Arragon, to Navarra, and
> hence even to Italy. . . . The scattered bits and pieces
> of Spain were thus gathered and joined into one single
> kingdom.

Notice the role of the soldier who forges a new world and creates a
new role for the cleric, the pastor educator, or the clerc.

> So far this language of Castilla has been left by us
> loose and unruly and therefore, in just a few cen-
> turies, this language has changed beyond recognition.
> Comparing what we speak today with the language of
> 500 years ago, we notice a difference and diversity
> that could not be greater if these were two alien
> tongues.

Please notice how in this sentence language and life are torn asunder.
The language of Castilla is treated as if, like Latin and Greek, it
were already dead. Instead of the constantly evolving vernacular,
Nebrija is referring to something totally different: timeless colloquial. He clearly reflects the split that has come into Western perception of time. The clock had come into the city, had been lifted
onto a pedestal, had been made to rule the town. Real time, made

up of equal pieces of equal length no matter if it was summer or winter, had first come to dictate the rhythm in the monastery and now began to order civic life. As a machine has governed time, grammar shall govern speech.

But let us go back to Nebrija:

> To avoid these variegated changes I have decided to
> . . . turn the Castillan language into an artifact so
> that whatever shall be henceforth written in this lan-
> guage shall be of one standard coinage that can out-
> last the times. Greek and Latin have been governed
> by art and thus have kept their uniformity throughout
> the ages. Unless the like of this be done for our lan-
> guage, in vain your Majesty's chroniclers . . . shall
> praise your deeds. Your labour will not outlast more
> than a few years and we shall continue to feed on
> Castillan translations of strange and foreign tales
> (about our own kings). Either your feats will fade
> with the language, or they will roam among aliens
> abroad, homeless without a dwelling in which they
> can settle.

Please notice how Nebrija proposes to substitute for the vernacular a "device," an "artificio." Unruly speech shall henceforth be sub-stituted by standard coinage. Only 200 years earlier, Dante had still assumed that any language that had been learned and that is spoken according to a grammar could never come alive. Such lan-guage, according to Dante, could not but remain the device of schoolmen, of "inventores grammaticae facultatis." Nebrija has a different perspective on power and rule. He wants to teach people the language of clercs, to tighten their speech and to subject their utterances to his rule. For Isabela the Queen, language was per-ceived as a domain. For her, the vernacular is the domain of the present, the utterance in which every speaker is sovereign. For Don Antonio the grammarian, language is a tool that serves, above all, the scribe. With a few words, he translates his "dream of reason" into a monstrous ideology, the supposition on which, hence-forth, the industrial system shall rise. Artifact shall substitute autonomous subsistence; standard shall replace unruly variety; predictable outcomes shall remove the risk of surprise. He presses language into the service of fame—more precisely, of a new kind of fame that is best called "propaganda."

> I want to lay the foundations of that dwelling in which
> your fame can settle. I want to do for my language

> what Zenodotos has done for Greek and Krates for
> Latin. No doubt, their betters have come after
> them. (But to have been improved upon by their
> pupils) does not detract from their, nay from our,
> glory to be the originator of a necessary craft, just
> when its time had become ripe; and, may you trust
> me, no craft has ever come more timely than grammar
> for the Catillan tongue.

In only a few lines, Nebrija spells out the sales talk of the
expert to his government that henceforth becomes standard: Majesty,
you need the engineer, the inventor who knows how to make out of
your people's speech, out of your people's lives, tools that befit
your government and its pursuits. No doubt, believing in progress,
I know that others will come who shall do better than I; others will
build on the foundations that I lay. But, watch out, my lady, you
cannot delay accepting my advice: "This is the time. Our language
has indeed just now reached a height, from which we must more
fear that it slide than we can hope that it ever shall rise." Already,
the expert is in a hurry. Already, he blackmails his patron with the
"now or never" that leads to so many modern policy decisions. The
queen, according to Nebrija, needs the grammar now, because
soon Columbus shall return.

> After your Majesty shall have placed her yoke unto
> many barbarians who speak outlandish tongues, by
> your victory these shall stand in new needs: in need
> for the laws that the victor owes to the vanquished
> and in need of the language that we bring. My grammar
> shall serve to impart to them the Castillan tongue as we
> have taught Latin to our young.

We know well whose concept of language won out: language
became one more tool managed by the professional lackey to power.
Language was seen as an instrument to make people good, to make
good people. Language became one of the major ingredients put by
the hermetic alchemist into the formula by which new men were
made to fit a new world. Mother tongue, as taught in the church
and the classroom, replaced the vernacular that mother spoke.
Mother tongue became a commodity centuries earlier than mother's
milk. Men took charge of the "educatio prolis," shaping Alma
Mater as their social womb and breast. In the process, the sovereign subject became a citizen client. The domination of nature and
the corresponding improvement of people became central public—
supposedly secular—goals. "Omnibus, omnia, omnino docendi ars"—

"to teach everybody everything totally"—became the task of the educator, as John Amos Comenius spelled it out in the title of his book. The sovereign subject turned into a ward of the state. The doctrine about the need for primary education for the exercise of citizenship destroyed the autonomy of Isabela's subjects: she could tax her subjects, force them to work on the streetgang or call them into the army; she could not question their dignity as the teacher can.

The Age of "Uniquack"

The third mutation in the vernacular has happened under our eyes. Most people born before World War II, rich and poor alike, learned most of their first language either from persons who spoke to them, or from others whose exchanges they overheard. Few learned it from actors, preachers, or teachers, unless that was the profession of their parents. Today, the inverse is the case. Language is fed to the young through channels to which they are hooked. What they learn is no more a vernacular that, by definition, we draw into us from roots that we send out into a context in which we are anchored. The roots that serve for this purpose have become weak, dry, and loose during the age of schooling, and now, in the age of life-long education they have mostly rotted away, like the roots of plants grown in hydroponics. The young and their linguists cannot even distinguish any more between the vernacular and the high-class slang that they take to be "gutsy." Language competence now, to a large degree, depends on sufficient supply of teaching.

The lack of personal sovereignty, of autonomy, appears clearly in the way people speak about teaching. At this very moment I am talking to you, and in another four minutes I will be speaking with you, when the time for discussion will have come; but neither now, nor then, will I be teaching. I am arguing a point, presenting to you my opinions—perhaps I am even entertaining you. But I refuse to be pressed by you into your service as a teacher. Much less am I educating you. I do not want anything to do with that task for which nature has not provided me with the necessary organs. I have told you, perhaps, about some facts that had escaped you about the Abbey of Gorz or the court of the Catholic kings; but, believe me, it was done without any intent at shaping or rapping you for the sake of education. And I hope that I have convinced you that it is more than a terminological nicety when I insist that teaching is a very peculiar, always hierarchical form that conversation in the vernacular sometimes takes. Unfortunately, many of our contemporaries cannot grasp this any more. Language has become, for them, a commodity, and the task of education that of training language producers by equipping them with a language stock.

A short while ago I was back in New York in an area that two decades ago I had known quite well: the South Bronx. I was there at the request of a young college teacher who is married to a colleague. This man wanted my signature on a petition for compensatory prekindergarten language training for the inhabitants of a slum. To overcome my resistance against this expansion of educational services, for a whole day he took me along on visits to brown, white, black, and other so-called "households." I saw dozens of children in uninhabitable high-rise slums, exposed to all-day TV and radio, equally lost in landscape and in language. My colleague tried to convince me that I should sign the petition. And I tried to argue the right of these children for protection against education. We simply did not meet. And then in the evening, at dinner in my colleague's home, I suddenly understood why: this was no more a man but a total teacher. In front of their own children, this couple stood "in loco magistri." Their children had to grow up without parents—because these two adults, in every word which they addressed to their two sons and one daughter, were "educating" them. And since they considered themselves very radical, off and on they made attempts at "raising the consciousness" of their children. Conversation has turned for them into a form of marketing—of acquisition, production, and sale. They have words, ideas, sentences; but they do not speak any more.

Gregory Anrig

4

EDUCATION IN CHINA

Other than some study of the Far East when I was in graduate school and service in Korea during the war, my experience with the Far East is limited to 18 days in the People's Republic of China in November 1977. So I want to immediately disclaim any expertise. I can only tell you what I saw in those 18 days, and even that is limited by the fact that we were guests of the government, so what we saw was what the government wanted us to see.

Let me start by describing a Chinese school to you, just to cast the setting. At best it's a stucco building—one or at most two floors, lights are very poor—perhaps a dangling light in the middle of the classroom, and no modern technology at all. The room is heated by a stove in the middle of the classroom and the kids come to school very warmly dressed—they have longjohns on at all ages—mainly because that's the only way to stay warm in the cold classrooms. Most of the classrooms have windows, but some of them don't. The setting is as dark, unattractive, unelaborate, and unmodern as one can imagine. There is a blackboard up in front and double rows of fixed desks going back. One of the things that strikes you most as you visit a Chinese classroom is that the average class size is about 45. That just wouldn't happen with our collective bargaining contracts over here; Chinese teachers don't have collective bargaining.

Despite these conditions, however, it would be a mistake to say education in China is terrible, because we found that education—in view of their purposes—was very effective and very impressive. It's a country of almost 900 million people (in fact, nobody quite knows how many at any point in time), but they have apparently managed to establish universal elementary education for the entire population and secondary education for most of the population. They

63

have, in short, made a remarkable accomplishment in a country that's immense. Their educational system includes—for example, out in the frozen tundra—teachers on horseback who, like itinerant preachers in our earlier days, go around from village to village and may only get there once a week, or once every two weeks. For those people who live on river boats—and many people do in China— they have somebody who comes around in a boat and teaches. They have done an extraordinary job of reaching out and trying to deliver education to their population. There's a reason for that. Education in China is a matter of national policy. It's not, as in this country, something that's left for the states—or in that country, to the provinces. It is part of their national objective to have elementary and secondary education in the countryside.

NATIONAL GOALS AND CLASSROOM PRACTICE

One of the things that impressed me about what I saw was the consistency of what takes place in the classroom in terms of meeting national objectives. It's wrong for us to go over there and say that, in comparison with American schools, they don't do certain things very well. The function of Chinese schools is different from that of American schools. So I tried not to jump too quickly to judgments about their schools, since they have such different purposes. I remember one night we were meeting with a provincial chief, who is a counterpart of our state commissioner. (The provincial chief responsible for the entire Shanghai area, by the way, is a woman. Very frequently, the top leaders we met were women, which I thought was an area in which they are way ahead of us.) One of my counterparts from Texas, a state commissioner down there, read to her from the "Educational Goals of Texas," which are not much different from the educational goals you will find in any other state document: to fulfill individual potential, hopes, and aspirations for the future, and develop personal, social, and educational skills. Then, he said, "Now, I've just read that to you from the Texas Bulletin. Aren't these the same goals you have here in Chinese schools?" And this woman, who is a remarkable human being, just sat there with her feet hardly touching the floor—she was so small— and she just shook her head. So we said, "What are the goals of schools in the People's Republic of China?" She said that the goal was to develop productive workers with socialist consciousness. And those goals are reflected in the schools everywhere you go. Wherever you visit a school in China, that theme is built into what is going on in the school—productive workers and socialist consciousness.

The thing that impressed me the most was the consistency between national policy and classroom practices. I wish we could have such clear ties between what we say we're about in public education in the United States and what you observe in the classroom. Quite often in America our classrooms are inconsistent with what we say in educational policy statements. In China there is a high degree of consistency between what they say they want from their schools and what you actually see as you visit schools and watch what's going on in the classroom.

One of the key things that I found in China—and this is a sharp contrast to our country where we pride ourselves on keeping politics out of the classroom—is that politics there is in command of the curriculum. The schools exist to carry out national policy, and that policy comes through in a number of ways. You don't go into any classroom, as dismal as it may be, without two pictures up front—and those pictures are of the late Chairman Mao and Chairman Hua, the current chairman. Their color pictures overlook every room in every school, and it's clear that they are watching you and that what you do ought to be what they expect of you. A second thing that you will find is that teachers are constantly reinforcing the political themes. For instance, I went into a classroom where they were teaching English to Chinese elementary students, and the youngsters would stand up in a rather uniform way and say, "I want to be a worker," or "I want to be a peasant," or "I want to be a soldier." And the teacher would always reinforce it by saying, ". . . to better serve the people." Wherever you went you would hear these same themes, and it was not so much a broken record as it was clear and consistent—getting the message across all the time. It may seem trite to keep repeating the Party Line, but in effect they are getting the line across to people on a steady basis in everything they do. It's a part of the politics being in command of the curriculum. In all aspects of what goes on in the school there is a reinforcement of the national goals and slogans.

The blackboard in America, for example, is used for instruction. In the Chinese school it is also used for instruction, but most of it is filled up with slogans. As you sit down in any classroom, up there right before your eyes all the time will be a series of slogans, and they're either quotations from Chairman Mao or some of his poetry, or party exhortations to study hard, work hard, and be loyal. If you look at the walls of the building, there are posters up with the same exhortations. It is a constant, steady—not heavy—drumming in of the themes that the society expects of its young as they move through school. It's a very effective form of education. One could say it's brainwashing, and indeed it is that. One could say it's indoctrination, and indeed it is that. But it's also teaching and it serves a purpose. If we look at it from our perspective, we'd say that's a terrible way to teach children. But from their perspective, it's serving the national goal—to take a country of 900 million people and have some unity, a sense of direction, and a sense of mutual responsibility—which is a very important part of what they're doing.

Elementary and secondary schools in the People's Republic are in session six days a week for about seven hours a day. It's a long, long day. But on Wednesday and Saturday afternoons the students leave the classroom and engage in extracurricular activities. During that time the teachers engage in political education. So it's not just what goes on in the classroom; there's also a constant reinforcement of the political themes with the teachers as a group as they go through their entire careers. You never have enough political education, and it's a scheduled part of the teacher's assignment to have these hours for political education, primarily on Wednesday and Saturday afternoons. The same thing is done to the teacher that is done to the student: a constant reinforcement of what are the expectations of teachers in Chinese society.

We went into a kindergarten classroom, and there they had a table model of a commune. This happened to be an agricultural commune, but there are also oil and industrial communes they speak of very highly. The students were learning their lessons from this model commune. When they studied math they studied how the Tai Ching commune met its production goals—again, the reinforcement of not only math but production goals that are expected of a good commune. When they studied organization or social studies, for instance, it was in the context of the Tai Ching commune and how it operates well and governs itself effectively, and therefore is able to meet the national goals that are set for it—not only the production goals but other goals as well. So there is a constant effort to reinforce certain themes, certain expectations, throughout the Chinese classroom.

Another aspect of Chinese curriculum that I found fascinating is that there is a national work ethic—everybody works, everybody is a worker. As you go through education in China you must have work experience, and that starts in the nursery school. There is some task that every student must perform, and that is part of his or her identification with being a worker. The reason isn't to learn a job or career or to develop your choices as to what job you want to have in the future, but that you should feel an identity with the workers of the country. So work experience over there in the elementary and secondary curriculum is different from that in America. We try to help the student make an intelligent choice as to what type of work he or she wants to do. Over there the goal is to be able to

identify with the workers of the country, and that is constantly reinforced. It doesn't matter what you do: the important thing is
that you work, that you're doing something for others. For example, in one of the kindergartens we visited, the children started
assembling boxes at a certain time each day, and they did it in
assembly-line fashion. One would fold the ends, another one would
fold the sides, and they would put it together and pass it on to the
next one, who would put them in a box to stack them. These little
boxes that they were folding were for toys. When they finished in
the kindergarten, they sent those boxes to the nearby toy factory,
and toys were put into them and shipped out. So it wasn't "make-
work," it was real work. The assembled boxes that those kinder-
garteners made each day—and they had a goal of so many to do—
were sent to a factory and used. And they took that very seriously.
This was not a fun time for them, it was serious work. Again, it
was a sense of not just doing work, but fulfilling a national goal.
There was a certain pride even in these little youngsters in going
about their tasks, and I must say that they did it very efficiently.
I was impressed with the way they passed the boxes on to each
other. Of course, all of this must be qualified by the fact that we
were visiting schools that were used to having visitors, and that the
government wanted us to see.

Frequently, when you visited a middle school (which is what
they call their junior and senior high schools) you would see a factory on the site of the campus. It would be a processing factory or
manufacturing factory where students, as a part of their curriculum,
were scheduled to go and work along with the workers. The workers
had a responsibility to teach the students who came. You would see
them working side by side in the factory, whether it was drilling on
a machine lathe, or assembling watches. The school was identified
with the factory and the students all had the responsibility to go to
that factory and do some work. In the rural areas most of the work
experience had to do with going out into the field. There were times
of the year when everybody left the school and went out to work in
the fields. On a tea commune that we visited, the plant where they
processed the tea was right next to the school, and the students
would work in the processing plant.

Again, I was impressed with the consistency between national
priorities and what happens in the schools. China is a country that
is based on mass labor—it is not an industrialized country. They've
got to have people who are willing to go out and work at very difficult
tasks—for example, in the rice fields. There is an expectation set
at the earliest years that everyone has a responsibility to work and
contribute to society, and it is done with great spirit. Some of the
older students march out of the fields, maybe a hundred of them at

a time, and if they have met their production goal they carry special flags. I might say, by the way, that unlike our history with the WPA, I saw very few people leaning on their shovels, and that's something they couldn't have controlled. That is, there is no way they could have had a hundred people out there and everybody working hard simply because we were driving by. They were all working, and I think it was because of a sense of group. You didn't sluff off, because that would be disrespectful of the group.

One of the other things that impressed me about the Chinese schools was that they continued to stress their revolutionary roots. That troubled me a little because we're a revolutionary country too and yet, except for our 200th birthday, we never remind ourselves of that. But in China everything constantly is reinforcing the fact that they have come through a revolution and that they're still in the midst of a revolution. In an English class, for example, they had two posters in the front of the room: one showed a farm scene and a city scene before Liberation, and one showed a city scene and a farm scene after Liberation. You saw hovels and drainage ditches before Liberation, and you saw nice houses and sanitary conditions after Liberation; in the city scenes you saw similar kinds of parallels. They were learning English, but at the same time the Party Line was getting across that things were terrible before Liberation and that things are much better now after Liberation.

In general I found people working very hard, and my sense was that this was because they expected to work hard because they thought that was what was expected of them and they wanted to meet that expectation. I didn't find or sense the alienation that you sometimes see, for instance, on an assembly line in Detroit. I found people who were not grudgingly working; they couldn't have worked as hard as they were if it were grudgingly. There weren't supervisors walking around saying, "Hey, get moving, you're going too slow." The workers were self-disciplined. There was a self-discipline to the process that I found very impressive, particularly in the mass operations. There were no overseers walking around seeing that things got done. It was a form of group discipline that was involved. It wasn't a matter of getting people to sing the Communist anthem or anything like that. You may see that in movies, but I didn't experience it at all. It was more a matter of the seriousness of the country. They are about the modernization of a massive country, and they're very serious about it, very clear about it, and—from what I could see—very committed to it. That seriousness was very impressive to me, and I found it in a factory where, for example, somebody would be working for a very long time at a machine lathe. I found it in textile mills where the lighting was terrible and I couldn't understand why everybody didn't wear glasses. People were working very, very hard, not because some-one was standing over them but because they thought they should be working very hard. That ethic has been woven into the society and it's a very impressive thing to observe.

SCHOOL AND SOCIETY

We talk a lot here about community involvement—that it's good to have community involvement in the schools. I think you know, and I know, that when you check that out, there's not really very much community involvement in our public schools. In fact, if the community gets too involved, the people in the schools get very uptight. In China, I sense that there is much more interchange, much more of a sense of the school being a part of the community and vice versa. Older people, for instance, are invited into the schools, not just to be aides, but because they lived in the period before Liberation and they provide an oral history. The older people are invited in to talk about "before the Revolution" and then to talk about the present, and these grandparents are, in effect, teachers. They experienced the pre-Liberation and post-Liberation periods and they're encouraged to come in and talk to students about the differences. In the neighborhoods, one family is designated to be the neighborhood center at night, and five or six youngsters will go to that family with the expectation that the mother and father will help with homework. The students simply go to a little cottage where the designated family has a responsibility to help with the homework of the five or six youngsters in the immediate neighbor-hood. Again, a close link between the school and the neighborhood. I visited a family, by the way, that had a little plaque up on the apartment wall. This was an elderly woman who had been helping schools on a regular basis, so she got a certificate which was up on her wall, and she was very proud about that certificate. She didn't get any money for it, but it was her duty and she did it, and got a great deal of pride and satisfaction out of it.

They have a small amount of military drill in the schools, all the way from the earliest grades up through graduation from middle school. Soldiers from the People's Liberation Army come to the schools to conduct the military drill, so again there's a tie with the society rather than a feeling of separation from it. A soldier comes and teaches the students how to make up their packs, how to march, and the importance of discipline and obeying orders. And they go on field trips. It was interesting that military training was the one area we were not told about; it sort of slipped out. We pursued it and it turned out that every school does have military drill, but they really didn't want to make a point out of that. They were talking about a lot of other things, but that one we had to pull out of them.

We also found that the children had a very extraordinary amount of skill in music and dance. Every school that we went to would put on a performance for the visiting delegation as we left. Most of the Chinese are usually dressed in very drab clothes—it was a question of whether you wore navy blue or gray and usually a Mao jacket—though this was not the case for small children. These youngsters would come out in very elaborate, colorful costumes. They would do dances, sing, and do acrobatics in a way that I don't see in the American schools. They put a great stress upon personal performing skills at a very early age, and these children had extraordinary stage presence. It wasn't the kind of embarrassed performance where we get out on the stage and shuffle our feet a little bit. These youngsters got out there and looked the audience straight in the eye, and then put on a really polished, self-confident show. You really had a feeling you were seeing Ethel Merman all over the countryside!

I couldn't quite understand why there was so much of this, and then I began to realize that the children go to school six days a week, seven hours a day, and their classrooms are strictly disciplined. The teacher directs the class and the students sit quietly. When they're called upon, the students stand, answer, and then sit down again. When they're not being called upon, the children sit with their hands behind their backs, leaning back on their hands, and that's how elementary school youngsters spend the whole day. Well, if children have that long a day, and if the academic portion of their day is that rigidly disciplined, they have to have some break from it. What they apparently do is schedule music, dance, and physical education throughout the day as a way of breaking from that strict discipline. I found that in contrast to the academic classes, which were the height of traditional education, the music, physical education, and dance classes were very free-flowing. They involved a lot of activity, lots of noise, lots of laughter, lots of movement, and none of the discipline you see in the academic classroom. The result is an extraordinary degree of stage presence and delightful artistic capacity in these kids.

I have already mentioned that children don't go to classes on Wednesday and Saturday afternoons. That's a time when they go to extracurricular activities. In contrast to our country, where extracurricular activities, unfortunately, are on a down-turn, in that country the extracurricular activities are scheduled as a very important part of the curriculum and people are hired separately to conduct them. In Shanghai, for instance, they have what they call the "Children's Palace," and students are selected from all over the city of Shanghai to go there on Wednesday and Saturday afternoons. Everything that you can imagine—from art to poetry, ballet, music, instrument playing, gymnastics, opera, health laboratory work, machine technology, and model building—is being taught on an extra-curricular basis by the finest of teachers. We saw some very extraordinary talent in the time that we were there. As with everything else, of course, no matter what was done, there was a political theme to it. The dance was with red banners—the heroic soldiers coming back from a victory; the poetry was "Free Taiwan." Everything that went on there had some political theme to it.

I also observed what appeared to me to be an impressive degree of sexual equality. The relationship between men and women in the official realm was, as far as I could see, straight from the shoulder: no paternalism and no maternalism. At every level that we visited there were women as well as men in positions of high authority. Their relationship with each other was a very respectful one. There would occasionally be corrections of one or the other, but it was always done in a very open and straight way. I later heard that my impressions were perhaps heavily weighted by what we saw—that they may have been deliberately showing off for us because there is still a lot of sexism in the society; but what I saw was extremely impressive. That also included the construction gangs, which always included women as well as men working at heavy labor.

My final point has to do with the role of teachers. While it is true that the classes are very traditional, very teacher-directed, and tightly disciplined, I'm very familiar with visiting classrooms and I can sense (as can all of you who have been in the classroom) what the climate is between the teacher and the students pretty quickly. You can tell whether the students are feeling repressed, and whether the teacher is insecure in his or her position. These are just things you sense—nothing you could put on a checklist—but you sense them pretty quickly. What I sensed in most of the classrooms that I visited were teachers who respected their students and students who respected their teachers. It was a very impressive thing to see because it was a very tightly disciplined situation, but it wasn't a forced or imposed discipline. The teachers we met seemed to recognize that they were important to national goals, and there was a heightened self-respect that came from that. There was no sense of inferiority—as there too often is in this country—but rather a real sense that what they were doing was important to their country. I was impressed by that.

I was also impressed with their ability to teach what we call "special needs" children. We kept on asking, "What about slow kids? You have a class of 45, how do you deal with slow kids? Do you group them or something?" They said they didn't because they believe that would do ideological and psychological harm. It would make a person feel that they were not as good as the others. Again, a remarkable consistency between national goals and classroom practices. So I asked, "Well, what happens if a youngster is having trouble?" And a teacher said, "Oh, it's my responsibility to work with that child and I'll meet with him afterwards. I'll go to his home and I'll work with him until he doesn't have those problems. And the other students help also." You have to remember that we may have been getting a little propaganda as we were going around, but my impression was that there was some genuineness to what they said. We sometimes wished we could find a way of transporting that attitude on the part of teachers over here without taking in their whole society as well. I was very impressed with the climate I found in the classroom. It was not one of caning, or of a dictatorial or totalitarian attitude. It was a very humane, concerned atmosphere.

We also noticed that as teachers and administrators met, it was not unusual for a teacher to cut in politely or to correct an administrator. If that were done over in our country, sometimes there would be that brief pause, as if something inappropriate had happened. But there was no such reaction at any meetings I attended. There was, again, that level of mutual respect. They are all engaged in something that is important to the national goals, and they didn't have a sense of hierarchy. That may be, in part, because the administrators are in some places elected by the teachers. But nonetheless, I found a refreshing lack of the sense of hierarchy that so often interferes with useful dialogue between teachers and administrators in America.

In summary, I would have to say I was most impressed with the high degree of consistency I saw between the national goals of the People's Republic and their day-to-day educational practices. How—or whether—we could achieve a similar degree of consistency, in view of our strikingly different goals, is a question I can't answer but see as eminently worth pursuing.

Jonathan Kozol

5

CHILDREN OF
THE REVOLUTION

In a way I am an odd person to be speaking at a conference on the future of education, because I've been so family-rooted and so stuck in the present. The farthest ahead I ever dare to look is to what you might call the middle distance. My inclination is to stay close enough to the present tense so that I can not only see the things I'm speaking of, but, more important, do something about them. So I am going to stick to rather practical matters. While others dream of structures of the future, I intend, instead, to speak about the water leaking through the rooftops of the present: the tenement buildings that our students live in, for example, and the water that lands too frequently on a kitchen or bedroom floor. It is quite a luxury, sometimes, to dream about the future. It frees you from needing to live in the present and from taking actions that are possible, risky, and realistic. Speaking about deschooling, for example, is easy; but it is harder to bring about those radical, and possible, changes in our schools that might make life ten times richer, and a thousand times less barren, for 50 million children who cannot drift off to a mountain top in Mexico, but who are required by law to go to buildings known as "schools" right here and now. So I'm going to cut my own suggestions to the bone and limit myself to the following few topics: testing, tracking, slotting, and applying labels; forcing therapy, administration of drugs, whipping, beating, racism, classism, sexism, and ethical problems in our schools; the issue of skills—why or whether we don't teach them any more; and Anglo-Saxon arrogance. After that, I'm going to go on briefly to speak of the wisdom of a man named Paolo Freire; weeks I spent in 1977 and 1978 as a classroom teacher in the schools of Cuba; a few virtues of socialism—I found that there were some; and a couple of minor problems with the capitalist system—I think I found a few.

INDOCTRINATION, OR "THE
SOCIALIZING FUNCTION"

To get right down to the real world in which we live and die—
or, too often, live the life of dead men and dead women long before
our epitaph is even read—I want to state what I believe are the three
essential changes that we must bring about within our schools in the
years immediately ahead. Once we have dealt with the prior and
obvious curse of racist, sexist, segregated education, the three
changes I have in mind are these: (1) An end to school as twelve or
sixteen years of a mandatory holding pattern—a postponement of
real life; (2) An end to school as twelve to sixteen years of mandatory, nationalistic, state indoctrination contrived to render us impotent and weak in the face of corporate demands and designed to
make us docile voters, manipulable consumers, and—in case of war
or crisis—willing killers; (3) An end to the school as the primary
instrument of socioeconomic class selection, tracking, slotting, or
whatever other label we prefer to use.

To deal with the second evil, indoctrination, is in a sense to
deal a death blow to all three. So I'm going to start right there.
And in order to do that, I will explain, first, what I mean when I
say "indoctrination," because a lot of people don't understand that
it is something that takes place here in the United States, just as it
does in almost every other modern, developed, Western nation. It's
odd that people in our schools of education always find it a surprise
when I mention indoctrination, because it's the only essential reason
for the existence of our public schools and the only basis on which
they were founded in the first place. But it's not surprising that we
avoid the term. We use that word for bad countries—Russia, China,
Cuba. We know that they indoctrinate their children in all of those
countries. But in the United States of America, in the double-talk
of our schools of education, we have much nicer terms. We call it
the "socializing function"—socialization—as though it were some
sort of benign and bland amalgam of love and trust and Elmer's glue,
ready to stick us all together as one people. Well, the words are
different, but the function is the same. It's 12 years of mandatory
self-debilitation, loss of passion, loss of anger, loss of soul. I'm
going to summarize very briefly what I mean by indoctrination in
order to make it a little less abstract. Before I do, I'd just like to
point out that I'm speaking in a really grand tradition. I'm not going
to base my statements on any radicals, but rather on good, patriotic
American citizens. Long ago, in 1844, Horace Mann made it very
clear that indoctrination was the basic purpose of creating a state
schooling system such as we have in the United States. The sub-
sidiary function of class stratification—assigning people to their

appropriate economic roles—is also well documented in statements
that have been made by many famous American citizens. Woodrow
Wilson is a good example. He said, back in 1909, "We want one
class of people to have a liberal education, and we want one class—
a very much larger class by necessity—to forego the privileges of
a liberal education in order to fit into specific manual tasks." That
was Woodrow Wilson. Never has there been a more honest and accurate description of the purpose of tracking.

What are some examples of what I mean by indoctrination?
The simplest and most obvious one is the Pledge of Allegiance.
Though I'm often labelled a "rebel," I like the American flag enough
so that I don't like to see it stained with lies, and the flag pledge is
a lie from start to finish. I have stood in classrooms in Detroit—
all black, all poor, all desperate—and I have heard those children
incanting this pledge to "one nation, indivisible, with liberty and
justice for all." It's not indivisible. It's not one nation. It's two
nations at least, very skillfully divided by the genius of our parents
and their real estate advisors and the banks. "Liberty and justice
for all," of course, is not the case. Liberty, for some; and justice,
maybe—if you can afford a lawyer like F. Lee Bailey, and even then
it doesn't always work.

The Grammar of Indoctrination

But the Pledge of Allegiance is obvious. Much more subtle is
the kind of indoctrination that doesn't <u>look</u> political, but is. For me
the obvious example of this subtle indoctrination is the English lesson, the standard English lesson, which tells you to avoid the use of
the first person. Public schools are scared stiff of the first person
pronoun, "I." Obviously they are even more scared of the first
person plural, "we." But they know that there can never really be
revolutionary solidarity until people first have had a chance to know
themselves. So, it's the first person singular that they set out to
destroy, and they do it with real skill. You see a silly example of
it in the grade school classroom. I don't mean to make fun of
women; it just happens that it is usually a woman in third grade,
and in this case it was: A teacher said something embarrassing. A
student said something rude. The teacher didn't know what to do in
the face of this rudeness, so she said to the children in a singsong
voice, "Is that any way to speak to me?" But the trouble was, she
didn't say "me." Instead she said, "Is that any way to speak to Miss
O'Brien?" The question is, Where is she? It's as if she left the
classroom—got locked in the closet with the chalk and the chalk
erasers. And, in a moral sense, the truth of the matter is <u>she</u> <u>has</u>
removed herself.

Now, if you're going to make fun of the third grade teacher earning 10 or 12 thousand dollars a year, what about the professor who's earning 30 thousand? The higher up you get on the academic ladder, the more elegant levels of alienation you achieve. In the third grade, you use the third person. Once you get to teach at the university level, you use the subjunctive. When you get your Ph.D., you use the conditional. If you want a lesson in alienation, go to the Harvard Faculty Club and listen to the conversations. I went there once for lunch with my father, and I listened to the conversation around me. There was a man sitting near us, at the next table, who had worked for years to build up to a "strong conviction" about something. I don't know what it was—I can't remember. In fact, at the time I couldn't even figure out what he was talking about, but the very fact that he had come to a "strong conviction" was really unusual in Cambridge. You don't get many "convictions" in Cambridge. Instead, you get lots of "notions"—like John Kenneth Galbraith, who seems to have a "notion" every Wednesday: "I had this rather interesting 'notion' about the price-wage spiral." No one is going to punch you in the nose for that. Can you imagine Malcolm X standing here in front of you tonight saying, "With all my heart, I will live and die behind this . . . notion." "Notion" comes from the Latin verb "to know" or "to observe." "Conviction" comes from the Latin verb "to conquer," and that's why you don't get many "convictions" around Harvard Square. In any case, here was a man who had a conviction at last. He was finally ready to present it to his friends, and this is what I heard: "One might ask, if it could be described . . . It seems at least within the bounds of reason to propose . . . One might suggest . . . There is a certain learned body of opinion that believes . . . It could, I think, be argued that. . . ." As if we were in a whole room full of third persons.

Or consider another example. A high school lesson that I saw a number of years ago included these instructions for term papers: "You will consult exactly fifteen separate sources: half books, half periodicals. [They couldn't make it sixteen for the sake of even division.] Take notes on four-by-six cards [not three-by-five] and be prepared to present them. Your paper will follow the MLA style sheet. The paper should have a clearly indicated beginning, middle, and end. [I have always wondered how you could avoid that. Could you write a paper with just a beginning and an end, but no middle?] Do not use the word 'I' except in the conclusion of your paper." So, essentially, you can't admit you were there until you're just about to leave the room.

Subjunctive, of course, is the verb form of hypostatis, and the third person is the pronoun of self-abdication. Together they constitute the ideal rhetoric for the man or woman whose hands are

skilled, but whose heart is dead and whose conscience is in exile.
It is the perfect training for the Vietnam bombardier, and far more
formidable for the one who sent him there: "Somebody else did it,
but not 'I.'"

The Myth of Progress and the Myth of Neutrality

I'd like to finish my definition of indoctrination by giving an
example from history. A lot of people think that history is taught
differently today from the way it was some years ago. The methods
have changed somewhat, but the content has remained the same.
The methods are individualized. The children come in and, instead
of meeting a teacher, they put on headphones, push buttons, and
plug themselves in. It's all individualized and made more appealing
by all the innovative styles, but the content is identical with the way
it was before. Remember a book called Streets and Roads? There
was a radical verson in the 1940s and 1950s called New Streets and
Roads. Then they went overboard in the 1960s with More Streets
and Roads.

And then came SRA (Stanford Research Associates) with individualized reading. As one black leader commented to me: "In the
old days, we used to have full-class indoctrination. Everybody got
it at the same time. Now, with SRA reading kits, we have individualized racism. Everybody gets it at his or her own pace." The con-
tents are unchanged. That's how our history is rendered more innovative. But the myth of progress still prevails and still goes
roughly like this: Each civilization is studied for its major contributions. You usually start with the Egyptians, whose major contri-
bution was the discovery of only two gods. Then the Hebrews come
along, and they discovered only one God. Then come the Christians,
and they discover the right God. Then comes Constantine (I'm skip-
ping a few minor periods of history here), who makes the question-
able decision to get himself converted. After which, as a seeming
result, the world slips into a period called the "Dark Ages," in
which it seems like progress has come to a halt. But the textbooks
won't have it that way, because if that were true the myth of progress
wouldn't be believed. So, instead of telling you that everything
stopped, they give you the feeling that everyone is resting and getting
ready for something big. Then, with the efflorescence of the Renaissance, they all burst out: from Martin Luther who hammers out his
message on the church door to all the outstanding painters of Northern
Italy. Then transportation joins the march of progress. This is very
important for the United States. Boats become ships, queens become
generous, admirals become audacious and sail westward to discover

the "new world." With the discovery of the United States—or what would become the United States—progress really comes into its own hour. Whereas before it happened only by eras, periods of influence, and generations, now it happens every four years.

Well, the evil in this lie—the myth of progress—isn't just that it allows us an idiot's optimism. The evil is that we are given ethical absolution by the myth. If everything is going to happen anyway without us, there isn't any need for us to put our bodies, our lives, or our careers out on the line and fight for something we believe. Why pay the price of struggle, risk, confrontation, loss of friends, loss of allies, or loss of tenure? Why, indeed, if everything good is going to happen anyway?

A lot of what I have just said leads to an obvious point. Why must education be confused with controversy and politics at all? A lot of people that I know would dearly love to think that education, ideologically and morally, could be both nonpolitical and neutral. It can't. It isn't now, it has not been before, and it will not be after we have finished with the struggles of our time. Teachers and students can never be neutral in the presence of an unjust social order. They either collude, connive, collaborate, or else rebel. Even if teachers never speak a word they are non-neutral by their silence. I'm non-neutral by the clothes I wear, the kind of car I drive, the kinds of friends I choose, the books I read, the neighborhood in which I have my home. Nor am I neutral, above all else, by the look of courage or self-exile that is written in my eyes. There is no way in which a teacher can be neutral, nor is there any reason why a teacher, man or woman, white or nonwhite, ought to try.

It's not a question of blaming schools or condemning individual teachers for the failures of the social order as a whole. It is the institutional function of the public school in the United States, and the nature of the values that this nation advocates, that we must struggle to attack, to change, and to transform. School is obviously not the only place where children hear these lies and learn these views, but only in school are we compelled by law to hear them and only in school are we brutally punished if we will not swallow what we hear. Life is too short, the world is too small, the bombs are too big, and the missile silos are too tall to allow us the luxury of educating another generation into a narrow, suicidal nationalism of the most stupid kind.

CUBA

I haven't time to give a detailed and adequate report of what I saw, and felt, and learned in Cuba. But I would like to speak briefly about Cuba because sometimes it takes a drastic shock, a change, a new kind of air, to make us rethink the positions in which we work and live. Paul Goodman once spoke of a "closed room of the imagination." That closed room is the room in which we are locked by the years we spend in public school. Sometimes it takes a really drastic shock to open up that room and let us even think of things on the outside.

I've been to Cuba a couple of times in the past two years, most recently in order to observe and then to teach within their public schools. I first studied the triumph of the Cuban government in eliminating illiteracy, as some of you know, by closing the schools in 1961 and sending students out into the mountains with lanterns and books to teach 1 million peasants how to read. In less than one year, nine months to be exact, a quarter million such volunteers—spearheaded by 1,000 youngsters—reduced the figure for illiterate adults in Cuba from 23 to close to 5 percent. Today the percentage of illiterates is more like two. This is not only the lowest figure in Latin America, but lower by far (according to UNESCO and the New York Times) than the present figure in the United States.

State and Revolution

Why did it work? For a fascinating and, in the long run, quite obvious reason. Not because the state gave up the basis of indoctrination in the course of education, because no state on earth will ever renounce that basis, but rather because the basis itself was built on liberation, not on acquiescence or docility or silence. The primer, the basic reading textbook that the teachers used, was not called "We Shall Learn Our Role" or "We Shall Learn Our Place," but "We Shall Overcome." And as a result, they did. As a result, the schools in Cuba today still do a brilliant and effective job of teaching reading skills. Not only in their language but in our own. Not because the bias is gone; as I said before, it never can be. But, rather, because the bias is in favor of change, of struggle, of irreverence, and of continuous regeneration of the revolution. In Cuba the word for the "state" is "revolution." While kids here might say "my allegiance to the state," instead, there, one hears young children say "my obligation in the revolution." There is, I think, a world of difference between allegiance to the state and obligation to a revolution. The latter means that one is a part of something that is still going on, so it is still all right to change.

This, perhaps, highlights two basic points about our schools. The problem, as far as I am concerned, is not that the public schools' prevailing interests are those of the state, since all public schools in every nation serve their states' interests. The question is, "What interests?" and "Which state?" In an unjust and unequal social order like our own, the interests are those of money and the state is an agency of worldwide exploitation and domestic havoc. The only role for an honest teacher in a state like ours is that of an earnest, skillful, and adept subversive in the most courageous, deep way. Certainly, the answer is not to abdicate our role. The opposite of dumb and brutal advocacy as we have known it for 150 years is not the teacher who tries to become a human version of an eggplant, the teacher who tries to abstain from taking any controversial role at all, the kind of teacher who doesn't want to be called "teacher." I've gone into many so-called "innovative" schools where I'm immediately given the now classic line: The principal says, "You don't want to talk to me, I'm just the principal. Don't waste time with me. Go down to room 12 and see Mr. McGoo. He's radical, he's innovative, he's wearing sandals, he has a beard, he's dirty, he's teaching in an open classroom where they're doing their own thing." So I look for the tallest person in the room, and I say, "Are you the teacher?" "Oh, no," he says, "We don't like to say 'teacher' in this school. I'm the resource person. The facilitator. We're all just learning and teaching together." I always think, if that is true, then he ought to share his salary with the children.

This peculiar abdication of the adult role is very strange. I've seen it at the high school level in a twelfth grade fiction class. I visited in November and I asked the students what they were reading. That seems a fairly nonprovocative question in a fiction class in November. There was a long silence. The teacher wasn't in the room. Finally one of the kids said, "Well, actually, we haven't got around to books yet." I said, "What?" "We haven't started on the books." I thought, if it was the last day of September or the first week of October, it might make sense. I said, "How come, what are you doing?" "Well, the teacher wants us to learn how to make democratic decisions. So we've been spending time discussing how we ought to decide which books to read, how to discuss them, whether we should have papers or exams . . . all the rest." I said, "Doesn't it get boring?" and the students said, "Are you kidding? It's so dull that half the class fails to attend. They don't show up. They stay at home and watch TV. At least on television—even on soap operas— there's a plot." One student finally said to me, "You know what I wish? I wish that on the first day of school the teacher got up in front of the class and said, 'This is a novel by William Faulkner, The Sound and the Fury. It's the best damn thing I ever read. Go home and read it. Come back tomorrow and tell me what you think.' You know, if we couldn't stand it—if we couldn't take all those long and endless paragraphs, and those hopeless sentences with parentheses

that start and forget to end, and the colons that don't lead to anything—if we didn't like it, we could have gone for Hemingway, or
Fitzgerald, or Doris Lessing instead. Or maybe we would have
loved it, and then we would have read ten novels more. At least we
wouldn't have spent the whole damn fall arguing across an empty
plate."

I use these examples to show that the opposite of bad schooling
is not no schooling, and the opposite of education based upon domestication is not the total abdication of adulthood, our passion, our convictions, our most earnest views. The opposite of education for
domestication is education geared to liberation. Not just liberation
from economic exploitation, but from docility, stupefaction, and
oppression of whatever kind. I found such an open atmosphere within
the Cuban schools: the power to criticize and to protest not just
against the obvious enemy for them—the U.S. government and the
C.I.A.—but also against the errors of the Cuban leaders, even the
minister of education, even Fidel. It isn't hard for Cuban kids to
feel the power to condemn Fidel, because he does it all the time
himself.

The Simulation Laboratory and the Workshop

Another feature of our schools that was suggested to me by
the time I spent in Cuba—and this to me is the most important one
of all—is something that I call, in the U.S. context, the "simulation
sickness." Some students call it the "as-if factor" of the public
schools. Our schools, as Whitehead long ago observed, are built
on inert ideas. Ideas that lead to nothing: not to action, not to
passion, not to transformation, but at the very most to good term
papers and examinations. Childhood is seen as a moratorium on
life: as preparation for life, but not as part of it. This, of course,
is one of the reasons that public school, for many children and many
teachers, is so damn boring. "It doesn't seem real," one student
said to me in Syracuse a few years back. Everything is like a simulation of some other thing out there in the real world. The ultimate
irony is the phenomenon called "simulation games." Schools have
by now excluded so much of the truth that, in some cases, they have
actually physically walled it out, as in Harlem where they built
PS201—the famous school without windows. Some said that it was
built without windows to protect the children from the unwholesome
atmosphere in which they lived, so that they could learn in school.
Others, more practical, said it was to cut down on windows being
broken by kids who didn't like the school, and some just thought the
architect forgot—which is probably the case. They spent 10 million,

20 million, 30 million dollars to construct this school, and then they spent 5 million more to imitate reality by use of complex, expensive games and gadgets manufactured at considerable profit by some of the major corporations, to simulate the world they had so skillfully walled out. So the kids end up sitting on the floor in the school without windows, in the middle of Harlem, playing a game called "Ghetto" in which they imitate what it would be like if, by some chance one day, they were to live in one of those sections of the northeast portion of the country known as the "inner core."

I was able to experience a very vivid contrast to this unreality the second time I went to Cuba, when I got to teach within a junior high school. The schools in Cuba, unlike those in the United States, are based on a very firm possession of the concrete truths of life outside. I mean by this that the ideas learned within the school are meant to lead to actions in the real world. In America when you are studying Latin they tell you, "Well, you might need it someday." But in Cuba the payoff—the action—the application of what's learned in school isn't postponed for sixteen years. It happens in the afternoon. I can describe this process best with a brief description of the kind of junior high schools that is now becoming standard throughout Cuba. They are five-day boarding schools where youngsters spend mornings in the classrooms in the study of biology, botany, zoology, chemistry, and the humanities. In fact, I found their academic training to be very rigorous. The students read books by Marx, Engels, Hegel, and Fidel—as you would expect. But many of the books were by Charles Dickens, Mark Twain, Jack London, Ernest Hemingway, and a lot of other good American rebels. It wasn't very different from the library we might find within a "good and honest" American school. They spend the afternoons out in the fields tending the crops, the dairy cows, the citrus fields, or the coffee trees. Each school is surrounded by 1,250 acres of land if it's a farm. The goal is ultimately to have 1,000 schools like these. The original goal was to do this by 1980, but because of the catastrophic drop in the world price of sugar and the consequent economic squeeze for Cuba, it probably won't be realized before 1985. Already, there are more than 600 of these schools and the one in which I taught was the first of them. You might wonder why I picked the first rather than the newest, especially since the new ones are really nice—with swimming pools, marvelous theaters, and all sorts of audiovisual equipment. But I picked the first one for an important reason. It was because of the name. The first of all the junior high schools in the countryside in Cuba was completed and dedicated in June 1970. The students that had been enrolled were present, the faculty were there, and Fidel Castro came out to dedicate the school. Being the first of what the Cuban Ministry of Education felt to be a

symbol of everything on which their education would be based, the
school was going to be named for Cuba's martyr hero—Che Guevara.
Instead, because of the moment—June 1970—and because the news
of student disruptions here in the United States had been so widely
dispersed by the media in Cuba, the students asked Fidel if the first
new school in the country could be named, instead, as a symbol of
solidarity with young people here in the United States. So the school
to which I went each morning to teach stands today under the name
chosen by the first 500 pupils in the spring of 1970: School of the
Martyrs of Kent. I wonder if there is any school anywhere, even in
the United States, even in Ohio, which stands today in memory of
those four young people who died by the shotguns at Kent State.

All of these schools are based upon a line of verse by a great
Cuban poet, a man often called the apostle of the Cuban Revolution.
Ironically, he wrote these words in New York City where he was in
"exile." Properly speaking, he said, "we should not say 'schools'
at all, but we should speak of these buildings as workshops for real
life. In the morning the pen, but in the afternoon the plow." There
are many ideas within the Cuban revolution that serious and reflective United States citizens surely find abhorrent. But it would serve
us well, I think, to take a good close look at the words of this great
man and at the idea of the pen and the plow which makes it unnecessary to bring simulation games into the Cuban public schools, because the real world is already there.

THE SCHOOLING SYSTEM

I would like to conclude with the most concrete suggestions
that I can for those of us who live and work here in the schools of
the United States. I'd like to speak briefly about some bread-and-
butter issues in our public schools that form a part of the total
structure of indoctrination: the education for domestication that I
have described. This includes testing, tracking, slotting, forcing
therapy, administration of drugs, and in general the entire mind-
set by which a single school or an entire schooling system can bring
itself to label those who are most likely to disrupt and to disform
the status quo as those who are "unhealthy." This same mind-set
allows people who cause the direct loss of life to other human beings—through denial of child care by school physicians, denial of
prenatal care, denial of needed funds for classrooms in our public
schools—to wander free along the highways of the nation. Who is
healthy, and who is ill, in a social order that has spent more money
in one month to kill poor people in Vietnam than it spends in an entire year to educate all of the children of New England?

Testing and Labeling

Our reliance on test data is another example of the schools' involvement in indoctrination to an unjust social order. I once taught two children in Boston, both of whom, if you believed the tests, had very low intellectual competence. One scored a 65 I.Q., I believe, and the other a 79. I thought both children were exceptionally bright. I thought they were gifted, and certainly their gifts and skills with me were unsurpassed. I thought maybe the tests were wrong. I remember tearing up the tests and submitting both kids, at their own request and that of their parents, for admission to two of the most fancy prep schools in New England. It seemed the only way out at that time in Boston, and the parents and children wanted it. In both cases, the schools—two very prestigious prep schools—did not want to accept the children. I didn't show them the tests—if they saw the tests they would never have admitted them—but recommended them on the basis of their interviews. They said the children were very nice but would be high risks. I remember my co-worker and I went out to the school to protest. We went to make a half-hour plea for one child with the board of trustees, and after four hours the chairman of the board of trustees said, "Well, we'll let him in because if we don't admit him, it looks as if we'll never get rid of you." So they admitted these two children and figured they would drop out within two years. Last year one turned down a full scholarship to Yale because he preferred to go to Dartmouth, and the other—from what I hear—is raising hell in her second year at Vassar. Not that admission to a prestigious college means anything very important in my own view, but it does say something about our trust in tests.

In the interim, until more is known about tests, are there any tests that work? Is there any test that is worth giving and worth our trust? It seems to me that there is one test: a teacher's judgment, very carefully and openly presented before the child and—at the elementary level—before the child's parents too. From this dialogue there might, perhaps, emerge the only judgment—the only test score, as it were—worth our respect. Until we know more about testing, this is the only test that I would trust.

I'm also concerned about the labels that are stamped on children's heads at the age of three or five or seven and left there for the next ten years. In the postal system, incompetent as they are, at least they finally have come up with removable labels: if you need to, you can peel them off. Not so with the labels of the public schools or, as we call them, "cumulative records"—the childhood version of the FBI's subversive file. It's not good enough that we set out to correct these files. What we must do is restrict them to absolute necessity. Render them open, at all times, to child and

parent alike. Forbid teachers from looking at these records, except for emergency medical warnings, until at least four or five
months of the year go by. And then make certain that all records
are destroyed for good in every school at regular intervals of not
longer than four years. This is only a start, obviously, but at least
it makes a dent in the perpetual damnation that is now made possible
by cumulative files.

Controlling

In general, the control of children through drugs should be
forbidden. In rare exceptions drugs of this kind should be administered, but only by a physician and only with the full consent and understanding of both child and parent. Understanding is important,
because too often drugs are used on children and people who speak
foreign languages and who don't really understand but are persuaded
to agree and sign their names. Those who illegally administer such
drugs, or who collude in such deception, ought to be seen as criminals and tried in courts of law.

There must be extreme caution that we do not exploit clinical
labels as simple devices by which to crush intelligent rebellion in
our most insightful children. I sometimes feel a sense of horror at
the thought of what adjustment counselors might do in the presence of
a child such as Gandhi, St. Francis, Pete Seeger, Helen Keller, or
Thoreau, not to speak of modern rebels like Jane Fonda or Ben
Spock. The child of conscience and ethics who imitates Gandhi and
Thoreau, who has the courage in the face of rotten textbooks to say
"no," is treated with clinical condescension—if not sheer and un-
qualified abuse. If he or she won't buckle under to the teacher's
or the principal's views, you know as well as I what we will do.
We'll send that child to the adjustment counselor in order to teach
him or her how to adjust to the unjust society in which we live.
There's entirely too much adjustment to injustice in the United
States, and people like William Calley and Richard Helms are the
direct results. We don't need any more people to learn how to say
"yes." We need more people with the courage of Dan Elsburg, Rosa
Parks, King, and Fidel, who had the courage to say "no." I would
propose we change the name "adjustment counselor" from this point
on to "disobedience instructor." I don't suppose that will go over
too well with school boards, but it seems to me it would be a good
change of names. The job of a disobedience instructor would be to
teach a child how, when, and why, by what means, by what logic, in
the face of what cruel orders, and by what successful tactics to say
"no" and not feel that he or she needs to build an instantaneous replacement every time.

You know the trap I'm referring to in that last point. The standard retort to criticism is, "It's all very well and good to criticize and break down, but can you do something better?" Take, for example, one of those reading books I was talking about before. The usual defense is, "A lot of people worked a long time to write these books for us, and draw the illustrations, and bind them, and print them, and bribe our school board into ordering them, and send them into our classrooms, and write a teachers' guide so we can learn how to get you to read them. It's all very well and good for you to criticize, but can you give us something better?" Of course, the stake in this is hard for the kids to see. First of all, what child in her right mind would <u>want</u> to provide something better? There are certain things that don't <u>need</u> a "something better." There are certain things that don't need to exist at all. It's as if, in the face of our protest of the Vietnam War, they would say to us, "Well, if you don't like this war, show us the way <u>you</u> would do it." The trouble is, once we accept that bind, we're trapped for good, and then we're frightened to say "no."

In general, the need is to make a clear distinction between healthy rebels, on the one hand, and genuinely destructive or self-hating children on the other. The latter are subjects for therapeutic help. The former, quite to the contrary, are the faint hope of our times. The world will not remember the good students who learn well the way to walk single-file in the hallways—and the way to march to war. It is the bad kids—the unruly, disobedient—like those who lived through all that blood and horror to form the Vietnam Veterans Against the War and then went on to fight against the proliferation of nuclear wastes and reactors, and like the ones who laid their lives down on that hillside at Kent State. It is these "non-adjusted kids," not those who build the bombs, who will redeem the nation's dignity in history.

Therapy, and in particular, repression in the guise of psychiatric care, must not become an ethical substitute for social change. Honorable protest must never be degraded by the facile aspect of the clinical eye. There are more books in print today about the psychological <u>causes</u> of dissent than there are books about the moral issues about which we dissent. In the face of the murders of the four children at Kent State we ask, "Why are the students in Ohio angry?" They are angry because their leaders are insane. Why are the Native Americans, the Blacks, the American Portuguese, the Puerto Ricans filled with rage? They are filled with rage because the treatment that we give them is outrageous. Indignation, rage, and courage are healthy and vigorous answers to the criminal behavior of the criminal leaders of an unjust and undemocratic social order. It is the children who, in the face of U.S. military sales and nuclear proliferation, can sit, smile, nod, and stare ahead who are the ones to cause anxiety in our schools and strike panic in our hearts. Those are the ones that we should send for medical advice.

HOW TO DEVIATE FROM THE CURRICULUM

A final question obviously is in the air: If I feel so strongly about these things, from what direction do I think some transformation will come? I'm one of those who feels that it is essential, while raising the largest issues, that we address the piecemeal struggles day by day. There's a slogan that grew up in Boston, around the beginning of the time that small freedom schools were starting in the country, that went like this: "Battles big enough to matter, small enough to win." It seems to me, in the face of the larger criticisms that I've made, that this is a good slogan with which to work.

One way I'm certain that change will begin is through the concerted power of courageous teachers, individual teachers throughout the nation, coast to coast. I have visited thousands of young people, older teachers, and student teachers in the past five years; in teacher centers, in small groups that meet often in basements of churches or in storefronts; both inside and outside of public schools, in established organizations like the National Education Association and the American Federation of Teachers, and from Portland, Oregon to Portland, Maine. I am convinced that there is a groundswell of effective men and women in this nation who are not afraid to struggle in the classroom to subvert indoctrination and domestication of the kind I have described, to risk their friendships and their tenure and, if it should be demanded, their lives. Fortunately a lot of these rebels are smarter than I was when I was teaching. I was a very dumb rebel. I got fired as a "permanent substitute teacher" within one year for the mistake of reading one poem by a black poet to a class of nearly all black children. It was called "curriculum deviation." But, lo and behold, within one month I was hired by the federal government to work on curriculum development! But nowadays there are many rebels in this country, in schools throughout the nation, who are much smarter than I was. These teachers who have the brains, if they read a poem that has guts and passion, not to mimeograph it and leave a sample in the principal's box. That's what I did. That's how I got caught. Fortunately, there are teachers nowadays who aren't as naive as I was and who are fighting at the grass roots level with a great deal of sophistication. There are thousands of such teachers. I meet them all over. They have guts and courage and they stick their necks out. There is much in the press these days to lead us to believe that the conscience of the

nation has gone dead since 1971. But there is much more conscience within the schools, the teacher centers, the networks, and
the free schools of this nation telling us that in the United States
revolution is alive and well. It isn't drawing massive crowds in
front of the TV lights, but—quietly and persistently—in every corner
of the land, the ethical determination of earnest, dedicated rebels
still survives.

If those I have met with in five years can gather their energies,
focus their goals, and even partially succeed, they have a chance—it
seems to me—to open up our public schools at last to a genuine competition of ideas. If the values of the United States can survive in
competition of this kind, then those values will be stronger afterwards. If our values cannot survive the competition, then perhaps
they do not merit the devotion of our children. They are odd patriots,
I always think, who do not dare to test out their ideals. There is at
the present time no free and open encounter in our public schools.
We boast that we have a free commercial market and a free press,
and yet that concept stops at the classroom door. There has never
been a free and open market of ideas within our public schools.
Perhaps this decade, the Bicentennial, is the ideal time for every
teacher to dedicate himself or herself to trying to make that concept
real: to turn around a 150-year-old function of the public schools
and to educate strong, ethical people first, and nationalist citizens
second, or tenth, or not at all. Public schools of the kind we have
today in the United States did not, after all, emerge out of the fore-
head of a god, but from the minds of vulnerable, ordinary human
beings like you and me. If they were made by men and women, they
can be transformed by us as well. The choice does not depend on
those who tell us our moral temperature at CBS and NBC. The
choice belongs to you and me.

Henri Dieuzeide

6

EDUCATION
AND DEVELOPMENT

We may wonder where to place this "future of education" we are gathered here to discuss. Has not the year 2000—which is so often proposed both as a myth and as a target for studies in the future—already been pledged? More than half of the decision makers, teachers, and administrators in education who will be active in the year 2000, have already been trained today. One may rest assured that, whatever futurologists may say or write, their own psychological inertia, combined with the stability of the system, will protect educators from promoting any radical change throughout their professional lives. In most industrialized countries, recruitment of teachers is coming practically to a standstill after the enormous intake of teachers called for by demographic pressures since 1945.

TOWARD THE TWENTY-FIRST CENTURY

The orientations we give to teacher trainers will have an influence on education as far as the year 2100—because they will train teachers until 2020, who in turn will teach until 2060, and their pupils will still be in active life in 2100. This shows that today's basic educational decisions may still retain their influence 120 years hence. It also shows how present the past can be in education: we ourselves are in a way a product of the year 1860. Indeed, there is a crying need for a critical evaluation of our present decisions in the light of what the future is going to mean. But, to be useful, we should not hesitate in setting our targets further ahead than the year 2000. How far?

This may not be easy to define. We should probably think in terms of a continuum rather than of fixed targets. Education establishes strongholds of the past in the future. Art, history, and science bring all the messages of the dead to shape the unborn. But who today is going to speak on behalf of the unborn? In education, as in natural resources, we are preempting the future and they, the unborn, cannot stop us. Can all those studying the future of education take provisional responsibility to stand up in their defense? How? Supposing they are willing to take this responsibility, are they equipped to do so?

If we were to establish a world map of futorological resources in the field of education, we would be struck by the enormous disparity between capacities available in different countries. The geographical index of the Guide for Organizations and Projects for the Study of the Future, published by the World Future Society in 1977, shows that practically all specialized institutions are located in industrialized countries, and that nine-tenths of them work in the United States on the development of American models of the future that are not likely to be accepted by most countries. Can American futurologists take the responsibility for all unborn children of the twenty-first century? Let it be said that we in UNESCO (The United Nations Educational, Scientific and Cultural Organization) are aware of less than half a dozen institutions working specifically on the question of the future of education for developing countries. The most active, to our knowledge, are located in India, Senegal, and Mexico.

Why have so few countries evinced interest in this field so far? If we look in retrospect at what has been said and written over the past 20 years on the future of education, now that part of it has become the present, we must admit that not much of it was reliable. In my contacts with various member states I have often heard charges of dilettantism, fictionality, or irresponsibility leveled against studies on the future, sometimes implying regret at seeing resources that could be better applied elsewhere wasted there. In most countries the status of studies on the future of education—their influence on the decisions of governments and educational authorities, on the behavior of teachers, and on the expectations of parents—is not high, and its impact is hardly felt.

This is not entirely the fault of those specialists dealing with the future of education, for there is little agreement among educationalists even on the present of education or the fundamental meaning of its tremendous expansion to date. Some view education as a passive subsystem of the socioeconomic environment. For others it is a powerful tool in promoting socioeconomic change. Yet others can only interpret education in a noneconomic perspective, as either passively reproducing the authority pattern and values of existing societies or as a forceful instrument for "conscientisation" and enrichment of ethical and cultural values. Was the expansion of education in the 1950s an automatic response to the requirements of economic expansion, or was it a strong social pressure originating in individual aspirations?

New thinking may be needed both for the present and future role of education in a worldwide perspective. This is all the more true in that there are, at present, signs of change of interest in UNESCO member states on the future of education. At the turn of the century, less than 2 percent of GNP was spent by developed countries on educational activities of any description. At present, developing and developed countries alike spend sometimes up to 10 percent of the GNP. For the past 20 years, assigning resources to education has been one of the top priorities of most developing countries. Now, all over the world, there is a slowdown on investment, although there is no explicit foundation for it. There seems to be a degradation in the political will of nations and their commitment to educational activities.

This reticence stems from the fact that education's relation to economic growth, employment, manpower needs, and reduction of social inequalities (to give only a few examples) is considered more and more by decision makers as a complex and not too well explored field of interacting forces often involving negative long-term economic, social, and cultural consequences.

This disenchantment is similarly reflected in the new pattern of thought that is gradually emerging in the community of nations and which is also being experienced in the UN system by reason of a wealth of studies, discussions, deliberations, and recommendations. These all incline toward the establishment of a new economic order between nations, a strategy to meet basic human needs, the launching of a "third development decade" devoted to identifying more appropriate models for development, a program of technical cooperation between developing countries, etc.

Such perspectives are no longer based on the projections of exponential growth of the early 1950s, but on considerations of the limit of physical resources (Club of Rome), on the structural crisis of employment (World Conference on Employment), and on the growing gap between industrialized and developing countries (New Economic Order—Group of the 77).

These views underline the dangers (or impossibilities) in pursuing growth as previously conceived, as well as the need to identify new strategies—not for growth alone, but for development conceived as a comprehensive multirelational process involving all the aspects of the life of a community, its relations with the outside world, and its self-awareness. It is worth noting that in this connection education is hardly mentioned (at least as a central element) by the 2000 year program, the Strategy of Basic Needs, or the Consultative Group of the World Bank. Indeed, there are many implications that nations may have to attend to more urgent tasks than looking at their educational systems. We may, in most countries, be entering into a zero-growth period for education, if not a period of decrease.

This is a very serious and new development in education which will certainly have important consequences for its future. Of course, it may be that educators in many countries will become alarmed and try to mobilize their forces to convince communities and governments to maintain their present efforts in traditional directions. It may be that we have reached the stage where new concepts and new strategies of education will have to be developed to cope with these orientations, for the new approach to development and growth has brought to light a new set of values in the international community, stressing such fundamental principles as self-reliance and protection of cultural heritage; integrated, balanced, and interactive processes of development; endogenous development and commitment and participation of populations in their own development. These now tend to be accepted norms for international cooperation, and the UN system would only consider futurological hypotheses that appeared to be compatible with them.

LEARNING FUTURES

Within this framework, some objectives of futorological studies in education become clear. If there are growing inequalities in international life, and if the ratio between capital income can be as much as 1:100 within countries and between countries, then inequalities in terms of knowledge and culture are even more severe. In developing countries there are more than 800 million illiterates and their number is increasing. In 1976 about 150 million children between the ages of 6 and 11 received no schooling. Inequality between the sexes in schools is still a reality in many developing countries.

Which kind of education of the future within countries and between countries would help reduce these inequalities? Where and what are the international strategies by which education could be developed and which at the same time would respect the diversity and the unity of the world? Though most world problems—human rights, peace, population growth, control of natural resources, economic development—are in practice closely bound up with each other, it is obvious at the same time that societies display the greatest diversity. Some of this diversity originates in economic disparity, but part of it also stems from deliberate efforts of countries to protect their identity, their language, their cultural characteristics, their way of life, and their interrelationships. How is international cooperation to contribute to the long-term educational construction of a society capable of satisfying the needs of its members in accordance with its accepted system of values?

One particularly urgent question is that of how to help newly independent countries to divest themselves of left-overs from educational systems of the former colonial powers and to successfully integrate their cultural heritage and modernity. A second question is that of how to reduce to a minimum the risk of being undemocratic or paternalistic in any long-term forecasting exercise that processes centralized information. How can participation of those concerned in designing their own educational futures be ensured? A third question is that of how to develop concepts of education into integrated, comprehensive projects that take account of individual satisfaction of basic needs, the national goals of self-reliance and cultural identity, and the international order with its implications in terms of international trade. At present these are reduced to a few quantitative parameters, the rest being abandoned in the face of the complexity of interactions and qualitative aspects of the development process and the radical changes it entails.

What use should be made of economic, sociological, and political theories in studies of the future? In what terms? The long-term future of education will look extremely different depending upon the approach adopted: conservative, based on manpower forecasting; reformist, aiming at planned structural changes; or radical, based on conflict, "conscientisation," or power theories.

Could we dream of studies that will develop an approach based on a minimal consensus—some kind of futuristic ecumenism—resulting in methods flexible enough to lead to practical solutions? For instance, most countries are at present faced with two opposing trends in education. One aims at modernizing, that is, at applying a model through programming, centralization, and rationalization of efforts. This application is based on the widest possible dissemination of standardized products, scientifically designed in order to generalize knowledge as quickly as possible on a nationwide basis. It feeds on the vision of a world inspired by competition and productivity. The second trend aims at revealing individual potentialities as yet unexplored, identified, or used, and is often called "conscientisation." This is based on new processes of interaction between individuals and the development within groups of their own values and objectives in order to unleash creativity and recognize divergences. Some critics of this second approach consider that the development of divergent, self-managed, learning microsocieties will inevitably become incompatible with the more authoritarian, national, scientific educational systems. To what extent will these trends coexist in the future? Can organization and innovation interreact better than they are doing now and fertilize one another and, by so doing, provide some models articulating formal/nonformal/informal education patterns of activities? There are signs that governments will invest more in activities of a less formal and more cultural nature, more decentralized and more community-based, whether in the perspective of rural or urban development. More long-term studies are needed in this respect to help countries better perceive the far-reaching consequences of their choices of today.

The search for the same basic consensus on learning futures could probably apply to such questions as these:

1. Since learning is not confined to schools, how can production activities of society be turned into sources of learning (bearing in mind the constraints of existing arrangements)? How can the use of resources and various educational agents be diversified, and the various pieces be integrated into a new system that would be an _educational_ system and not only a _school_ system?
2. Since new, variegated, and flexible structures are needed for lifelong education, how can coherence be given to the various elements of the educational system in order to ensure continuity, on the one hand, and mobility, on the other, each terminal stage being also a preparatory stage?
3. How can an educational system be devised that would better control interaction between science and society, and reduce to a minimum the destructive impact of technology on endogenous cultural values?
4. How can formal education, the school part of the system, be restricted to a few fundamental roles—learning to learn, developing creativity, relearning silence—and the incoming flow of additional functions be reoriented to other, nonformal sections of the educational system, such as the media?
5. How can maladjustment between education and employment and their future relationship (education for work—occupational training) be reduced?

International organizations could usefully undertake studies that involve their own future: for example, on the role of international cooperation and strategies of external assistance for long-term educational development.

"LIBIDO SCIENDI"

Let's be realistic: we are _not_ living in a world of harmony and peace. Violations of human rights, racism, apartheid, oppressed minorities, science and technology divorced from human

welfare, nihilistic feelings, violence, unemployed youth bereft of
the possibility to live in dignity, sales of armaments to poor countries, threats to peace—all of these are familiar problems. What
is quite clear today is the lack of social consensus or, rather, the
realization that there is no social consensus. "Delegitimization"
of leaders, parties, egalitarian aspirations, and self-management
are the order of the day in most countries. In education, in particular, it would seem that values that were the clothing of traditional
authority, such as "respect," "deference," and "decency," have
become obsolete in most cultures. Social relationships based on
violence and oppression, whether physical or symbolic, are more
clearly perceived and interiorized.

Dissatisfaction with schooling is only one aspect of this new
attitude. I do not think that refusal to accept individual failure in
schooling should be mistaken for a rejection of education in toto.
That there is no deference for teachers or no respect for school-
life conventions any more does not mean that there is no individual
aspiration for improvement. What strikes me, on the contrary, is
the frantic libido sciendi of today, the desire to know and understand, testifying to the formidable pressure to become master of
one's own destiny in developing and developed countries alike. One
is actually led to wonder if "delegitimization" of authority in many
Western countries and the hunger for schooling in the Third World
could not be two sides of the same coin. Lack of social consensus
does not exclude a de facto solidarity. If international organizations
cannot make up for the lack of consensus, they can help with solidarity. It is this de facto solidarity of mankind that studies on the future
of education should explore.

UNESCO is not a research institution or a university, but a
worldwide organization concerned with education, science, and culture. With 144 member states and 30 years of experience in intellectual cooperation and operational assistance to these member
states, it is in a position to facilitate a truly international movement
of studies on the future of education. The organization's program
includes two major activities in the field of future studies. One involves preparation for the International Conference on Education
which will be held in Geneva in 1981. A general report on prospects
for the development of education policies and planning in member
states during the coming decades, with priorities for international
cooperation in education, will be prepared with the help of a panel
of eminent educators, scientists, and specialists in culture. The
other plan is to convene an international conference of persons in
the fields of science and the arts in order to examine desirable
trends in the content of education for the future and to make recommendations to the international community in this respect.

This is an effort with a worldwide orientation and a global meaning. Groups organizing conferences such as this one on the future of learning could be associated with this new international program on condition that they are oriented toward a critical examination of worldwide evolution. UNESCO alone cannot reverse the trend, but it can help introduce the true dimension of the future—and what their education may mean for their future—into the thinking of most countries of the world.

It seems to me that concerted international action could develop immediately in four practical directions:

1. Intercommunication between institutions concerned with the future of education might be improved. Although interchange among some important people proceeds very well, the middle-level academic and research staff does the real work in isolation. Development of some kind of network would therefore seem to deserve consideration.
2. It seems that there is no methodological consensus, not even an acceptable typology of methods. An exchange of views, and perhaps some guidelines (if not a charter) might prove useful.
3. UNESCO could also foster development of autonomous research capacities on the future of education in developing countries, with the assistance of concerned research institutions.
4. In view of the fact that future studies have not triggered off serious international discussions on possible models (with perhaps the exception of the Club of Rome), UNESCO could assist in introducing a better international critical dimension by relating them to other research and training projects in the specialized fields of its competence. Such discussions could mean that the dimension of the future will at last be introduced in long-term planning and decision making in education.

Obviously, all these practical arrangements could contribute to the establishment of a working infrastructure that would bring about a confrontation of different futurological perspectives in education in different countries, on which UNESCO could then report to the conference in Geneva in 1981.

What is most needed is the development of calm, dispassionate studies capable of standing searching international discussion. Flamboyant opinions are not needed. What is required is a serious analysis of the long-term possible consequences of our actions and inactions of today.

Elise Boulding

7

EDUCATIONAL STRUCTURE
AND COMMUNITY TRANSFORMATION

I'd like to begin this talk about education and community change by sharing with you the feelings triggered by watching the last episode of the film "Holocaust." The experience kept me awake for a good part of the night. It was not what I saw in the film that kept me awake. I have been to Auschwitz, and I have had my wakeful nights over that. I've also had my wakeful nights in Hiroshima—sleepless nights that I'm sure all have when their imaginations dwell on what human beings can do to other human beings. What kept me awake last night, however, was the last image that flashed on the screen. It was the image of a young man who had been through the horror of the holocaust running to play ball with a group of junior high youngsters on a playing field. Nothing wrong with that, but what really struck at my life, as Quakers say, was that for a moment they froze on the screen the face of this young man running with a ball. His expression was one of utterly banal joy—a plastic image of joy. It was the typical football star happily dashing to victory. Apparently, all the producers of this incredible saga of human horror could think of as a climax for plumbing the depths of the human capacity to hurt and destroy was some kind of a smiling image that said, "It's all okay, folks."

That's what kept me awake: The need to hold up an image that says it's somehow really all right: that all the things we are doing are going to come out all right and it's really just a football match: we'll all take turns at winning—win a few, lose a few. The inappropriateness of that attitude to the social realities that had been dealt with in the film is a commentary on how out of touch we are with authenticity in human experience.

AUTHENTICITY OF EXPERIENCE

I want to speak of the need to recapture the authenticity of human experience—an authenticity which, by and large, our educational system as we now have it, and the social structures that support it, are organized to protect us from. Nowadays, for example, we can have secondhand knowledge about the whole planet and feel educated. That was never before possible in human history. Now it is possible to feel educated with nothing but secondhand knowledge. The other thing I want to talk about is the problem of developing enough perspective within our authentic experience to be able to speak directly about kinds of futures that will be radically different from the present that we know. The loss of authenticity of experience has been accompanied by a one-dimensionality of thought and life which makes us not really able to compare one type of social system with another, one type of behavior with another, one way of doing things with another. We have lost the capacity to make authentic evaluations of experience because of the one-dimensionality of the experience itself. Because I'm concerned about nurturing "futures-creators" of all ages, I'm concerned about how we reintroduce the opportunity to see the alternatives.

Futurism, in my view, begins with understanding the historical process. There is no way to understand the future by beginning today. You have to be in touch with the historical process. I'll say a few words about one of the most important parts of human experience, that which, historically, enabled people to create the beginnings of human settlements, and urban society, and civilization as we know it. I refer to the experience of nomadism. Once, we were all nomads. For most of human history, human beings have been nomadic creatures. People who change terrain on foot—not by car, not by plane, not by train, but on foot—have to be continually reading every aspect of their environment, because their survival depends on it. They have to know what's edible and what isn't. They have to know the meaning of changes in rocks, soil, bushes, trees, hills. They have to know what other living things are moving around them—what birds, what animals, what fish. There has to be, in other words, a very complex and continuous ecological scanning of environments in order for people on the move to survive. Humans got a very special kind of training through the many thousands of years of constantly shifting terrain—training in being able to choose camp sites, shelters, places where it was good to stay and where the best mix of resources was present. Everybody had to be able to make those choices and the observations that led to them. There was little room for specialization. Women had to know, men had to know, children had to know. There was continuous, very finely tuned observation of a constantly changing environment because the nomads didn't stay in any one place. Then, when those first settlements in the Mediterranean area began, each group that settled in a town began to lose its knowledge of what the larger world was like.

The settlement of cities—we've all been taught what a marvelous concentration of knowledge settlement made possible. What we've ignored is the loss of knowledge that went with urbanization. What happened, and this is documented in the history of empires in the Middle East, is that each new generation of leaders in the urban areas came from the nomadic tribes who invaded and settled in the city, but still remembered what the world outside was like. They knew how valuable their knowledge was, and provided a constant infusion of nomadic perceptions and experience into urban life. What the nomads had that the urban dwellers lacked was trained judgment; they could picture how things looked in different settings. If you can compare settings, you have a different ability to make judgments than if you have only known one setting. And so, generation after generation, the new blood came from the nomads.

The knowledge that came into those cities was a different kind of a knowledge than the knowledge you and I have. For example, recently I've spent a lot of time traveling. I've seen airports from Tokyo to Mexico to Los Angeles to New York. I have sat with a lot of different people on a lot of different planes, been in a lot of cars, and seen a lot of colleges, but what do I know about the terrain I have traveled over? The level at which I can make my judgments about the societies that I have passed through is inappropriate to the problems that underlie the human situation. It is an inappropriate level of generalization. Furthermore, as a college professor I am continually reinforcing this inappropriate level of abstraction by talking about social reality to students and colleagues who have less and less firsthand ability to map the social reality out there. We all contribute to this process of abstraction. Both children and teachers are crippled by the lack of firsthand terrain knowledge.

Another missing ingredient in our education that has been an important part of the human experience for gaining comparative perspectives is the firsthand encounter with "the stranger." The stranger can be the preacher, the missionary, the person who has been to far lands and comes back to tell you about people with strange customs living under tropical skies. We have vastly underestimated what it has meant for generations of children in all societies to have direct exposure to people who have actually experienced other ways of living. It is the one-to-one encounter of a child with a person who has been there. The child "sees," filtered through the voice of the stranger, a picture of what life is like elsewhere. It's the next best thing to the direct experience of nomadism. In autobiographies, as people remember back into important events in their childhood, the fact is repeatedly confirmed that the role of the visitor from far places has an impact on children out of proportion to the apparent cognitice significance of such an event. It is more powerful than hearing a lecturer from a platform, or watching a television show that recreates a jungle scene. Somehow, from the flood of cues that wash across the spaces between people when human beings share their own authentic experience in an intimate setting, something is absorbed. Some kind of internal mapping of the world takes place for the child as a result of that experience. We can try to replace such encounters by bringing visitors to the classroom, but it is not the same. There is something special about the dialogic nature of an encounter between a small child and a visiting stranger on familiar local turf. It could be a sailor, a peddler, a hobo, an uncle from afar—a stranger for any reason traveling under any kind of label who has this kind of impact on children.

Another type of experience that creates authenticity and that is not available for classroom experience today is the experience of growing up on a farm. When you compare what people know how to do who grew up on a farm with what people know who grew up in the city, the character of the knowledge is very different. Those who have had their teaching in the hay fields, on a tractor, in the vegetable garden, in the orchard, in the cow barn, and in the pigpen know things in different ways than do those who have had the best books and the best audio-visual aids. I recently interviewed some rural families in Oklahoma. Some of the teenagers from farms stress how uncomfortable they are in the city high schools because they know so many things that their fellow students in the city don't know. They don't know how to close that experience gap, because the things that they take for granted are just foreign to the city students. Rural teenagers, male and female alike, can make many different things with their hands. By the time they're seventeen, they can put together almost anything you can think of. But the city young people don't know how to do that, and put down the "country bumpkin's" skills. Most (though not all) rural folk have had an authenticity of experience, a training, and a competence that is just closed off for a whole generation of urban people.

Another urban-rural difference for children relates to something that happens in urban and industrial societies that I will call the "infantilization of a child," essentially keeping the child an infant. Over the world, generally, children enter the labor force at the age of five. By the time they are twelve, they are net producers— meaning they have already produced enough through their labor to pay back society for everything that has been invested in them, including the food that is fed them, and they are now adding and making surplus value. But in our society, these same children are non-persons until they are twenty-one. From the age of five to the age of twenty-one they are continually trying to participate and to use resources creatively, but no one notices, as if they were invisible people. In nonindustrial societies, because their hands are needed, they are noticed more. The children who grow up in our society are surplus personnel, so they are doubly invisible: no one needs them and legally they are minors until the age of twenty-one. Thus they suffer from the inauthenticity of being labeled nonproductive people who are good enough to fill schoolrooms, but not good enough to be shaping the products, customs, and social spaces of the society they live in.

THE EXPERIENCE OF ALIENATION

We have all these forces working against authentic experience. Yet it's not hopeless, because the alienation that this produces is, perhaps, valuable for the child. In some ways it may be lucky for the twenty-first century that the child of the twentieth century has been kept segregated from society. The alienation, and the marginal status it produces, can be a powerful drive toward creating a new image of the future. When we first started having children, Kenneth Boulding and I, what I worried about most was how it was possible to have our children grow up to be pacifists, peacemakers, nonviolent social change agents in this violent society. Some of our generation were very clear that we wanted a different kind of society for the future than we had in the 1940s and 1950s. Yet we worried about how it would be possible for our children, shaped in their growing-up by the present society, to develop and maintain commitment to an alternative future.

A study on conscientious objectors done during the war was very illuminating on these questions. The study exposed what brought these young people to a position so unpopular that they were labeled "yellow" and "cowards." "Unpatriotic" was the mildest word used. What made it possible for them to make such a choice? Some had grown up in communities where everyone was a pacifist, or in a historic peace church. For all those who had no such support, what made that kind of behavior possible? Each of the things that I have mentioned as paths to authenticity was found in the lives of these young people. Sometimes it was a stranger who came into their lives one childhood day: the child had heard words that created a mental image of something new and unfamiliar, not of that community. And that image stayed, became a part of them, and they chose another path, another vision, because of it.

Most overwhelming was the evidence—both in the material from the conscientious objectors and in the biographies I read later—of some powerful experience of alienation, of being different, undergone by the young person. A lot of the young men who went into conscientious objector camps had grown up in China, or Africa, or Japan as missionary children. They had come back to the United States as teenagers—back to the land that had been described by their parents as a beautiful homeland where everybody was good and kind. Idealizing the homeland is something that most people do when they have lived abroad for a long time. When teenagers, fed on these dreams of a wonderful United States where everyone was wise, generous, sharing, and democratic, confronted the reality of high schools in the United States in the 1940s, they had a shattering experience. They saw a lot of nasty things in American society, and experienced estrangement from the country they had loved and to which they had felt they belonged.

The trauma of alienation didn't necessarily come in that particular way, but every one of these young people had <u>some</u> profoundly separating kind of experience in their childhood or youth—perhaps nothing more than being very ill for a year, or moving to the countryside and having no playmates, or moving to a new town and being stripped of old friends. If somewhere along the way they had picked up messages about the possibility of alternatives, other ways to live and be, and if in growing up they had also acquired some measure of self-confidence, then they could take that alienation. They could deal with the pain in a productive way. We might say they became "futurists"—persons prepared to be creators of an alternative society.

Of course, not everybody who is alienated becomes creative. It is very important to identify those conditions of alienation that leave some space for the individual to "reach back in" and say, "I don't want to be connected with society as it now is, but there is a society I want to be connected with and I'm going to help create it." Our opportunity lies precisely here, as we deal with the alienation that young people are experiencing today. If we can identify that space left for "reaching back in to reconnect," then there is still hope for our society. Sometimes it seems that in our television-mesmerized society, with its high rates of crime and violence and alcoholism and drug use, we have reached the end of the line. But the other side of it is that the experience of alienation may have cracks and crevices in it where alternatives can be perceived; it may lead to the creation of a new society.

A PROPOSAL FOR A COMMUNITY-
BASED EDUCATIONAL SYSTEM

In thinking about how people can be helped to "get back in" out of the experience of alienation, I have envisioned the development of an apprenticeship system that would change the pattern of schooling in such a way that schools as we now know them could be completely phased out. The structures that we now have for school buildings would become headquarters for people of every age to use. The skills and knowledge of every person in a local community would be a part of a "map," and the local school would become the place through which people connect as teachers and learners. A five-year-old might begin apprenticing in a local park with the park maintenance personnel, or in a local automobile repair station, or a local drug store, or a local grocery store, doing the things a five-year-old can be taught. The same young person, at the age of nine, would be back at the same places doing very different kinds of things, and back again at the age of seventeen doing still other kinds of things. Every person in the community would be listed as a teacher. A person who is paraplegic, for example, is listed as a teacher of skills on how to survive with that condition. We already have found that prisoners are excellent teachers for nursery school children, so prison apprenticeships would be an important part of the program, as would hospital apprenticeships. (Persons would be apprenticed to prisoners and patients, not only to guards and nurses.)

In this concept, there is no space in the community that is not a "learning-site." There is no living, breathing human being who is not a teacher. And there is no age at which a person is automatically a teacher or a student, because five-year-olds can teach three-year-olds and thirty-year-olds. I would probably begin with those over seventy and under six in this system, because they are presently the most marginal people in our society and therefore the least threatening to the community as apprenticeship personnel. Then I would close in on the school system from each end: Six-year-olds with high school students, and seven-year-olds with junior high students. Eventually, you would arrive at a point where young people have been taught, and have been teaching, in every setting. Then you fan out to the community. If you think of a small town it may be easier to visualize such a system, but I mean this to apply to any kind of setting, urban or rural. Weaving in and out of what used to be the school semesters and graded classrooms would be concentrated learning sequences for particular skills such as mathematics, reading, and writing. The "three Rs" would be linked to apprenticeships as far as possible.

It would take a lot of people to coordinate such a system, because by the time you have identified everyone in the community as a person, a teacher, and a learner, and recorded the experiences they have had and what new learnings they need, you have a pretty complicated record-keeping system. Such a record-keeping system could either be some ghastly computerized caricature of all the things that are horrible about our society today, or a model of the "appropriate" use of high technology—enabling a person to chart a path through a very complicated society as a whole person, and to relate to other people as whole persons.

One important type of apprenticeship not easily available in our present society is apprenticeship to persons who are taking periods of solitude and withdrawal. This would, in effect, be apprenticeship to monasteries and convents and to hermitages in a brief, nonbinding novitiate. To learn what it's like to live a reflective life comes best, not from reading about St. Francis in a book, but from spending some days or weeks or months with people who are in a reflective stage of their lives.

Our lives are not of a piece. They go up and down and around in many phases and stages. An important part of the apprenticeship system would be to apprentice to all of life's stages while still relatively young, because that expands a person's image of alternative possibilities. What I envision is people knowing their community terrain in a setting of authentic encounter, and knowing the ground of experience of the skill of the carpenter, the pharmacist, the hermit, the teacher, and the young mother. (Apprenticing to young parents with newborn babies is another very important part of the apprenticeship program.) In each case, the skill comes with the wholeness of the person who teaches it, and the students must continually integrate all different kinds of skills. They would come to know a community in a way that no young people today grow up knowing their communities. No place would be inaccessible, no place would be closed to them.

This kind of community-based education could build up walls and create an ingrown knowledge that reproduces all the worst of what we have known in the past about village life. We must never forget that there was a reason people left the farms and small towns and went to the city: it was to open out the sense of options. But once you have arrived in the city, you often forget the original drive that brought you there and cease to keep the options open. So our task of redesign has to do, on the one hand, with reopening the local community for authentic experience, and at the same time, with creating a communication network that makes persons of every age continuously aware of their counterparts in the search for knowledge in other parts of the world. It would require the use of interactive computers and, of course, it would also involve a great deal of travel. Planes, properly used, can be an instrument of enlightenment. Badly used, they can represent the automated battlefield of Vietnam. Learning the appropriate use of computers can overcome the limitations of the fact that we can only experience a limited number of things firsthand.

Learning through Metaphor

This apprenticeship system would rely, partly, on concentrated teaching in the classroom of certain specific kinds of mathematical and measuring skills. But it would also require—and it's possible that the classroom could be a place to do it—instruction from a very early age in the use of metaphors for accomplishing the interior integration that is necessary because so much diverse experience is required of each person in this learning society. When I teach a class like the Sociology of Global Systems, which throws a lot of abstraction at a student who really has very little firsthand experience of the world, I try to find ways to ground these high-level abstractions in the firsthand experience of the student. For young children, such grounding is the most natural thing in the world. It must be continuously encouraged as they grow older. Such encouragement would include utilizing the fact that our bodies are very complex living systems: biosocial systems that we can experience firsthand.

There are many different kinds of bodily experience that can be evoked fairly simply so that we can have an image of the complexity of our own body. That complexity can become a profoundly important tool—experienced complexity that moves through ever more complex social systems. So I have invited college students— with younger children I would do it a little differently—to simply spend some time in awareness of their body as a biosocial system. Then I invite them to imagine that their body is the boundary of the social system that is their family. What that means is that one's skin becomes, in a metaphoric sense, the boundary of the family system. Such a metaphor can connect you with the complexity, the fantastic complexity, of relationships in the family. Given enough time to meditate on that, you have a different sense of the family and its relationships. Then you can move to the neighborhood that you played in as a child, and your body can be the boundary for that neighborhood, including the woman down the street who always scolded you for stepping on her lawn, and including the dogs and the children you liked and the children you didn't like, and the neighborhood policeman. Then you can move to the city, and the roads of the city are in your body. Your veins are the rivers; and the churches, the places of work, the stores are there inside of you.

These metaphoric statements in one sense can seem trivial, but in another sense they are not trivial, because they involve drawing on what we can experience in a primary way of the complexity of our world. The last metaphoric experience would be making your body the boundary for the planet. The mightiest rivers of the planet flow through you. The cities are located in you. The planes fly in you, including the Concorde. The automated battlefield explodes in you. The use of these metaphoric experiences has to be very careful, since the line between doing it in a way that draws on authentic human experience and in a way that makes another simplistic, plastic recreation—like the image at the end of "Holocaust" that I started out with—is very thin.

The Pursuit of Human Goodness

The longer I think about the task of education and the task of creating our future society, the more I realize that there is one thing that permits of absolutely no shortcuts. That is a commitment to human goodness, and the development and life-long pursuit of human goodness. Without that growth in goodness, as a part of the growth task of the individual and of the society, everything else can be misused. There is no structure, there is no text, no aid, and there is no technology that can protect us from a failure to seek goodness. One of the things that troubles me as we talk about futurism and social change is that we tend to adopt a language that assumes that if we use the right technology—if we use the right formula, organize classes right, give people the right experience—that somehow it's going to come out all right. We use a language of social transformation very glibly. But the kind of transformation that I am talking about is nothing less than a permanent process—a life-long process for the individual, a society-long process for a society—of continually evaluating and monitoring how we are doing, guarding as much as possible the authentic experience that gives a person the chance to make an honest evaluation. Without authentic experience, evaluations cannot have validity, and it is the evaluation process that is the most crucial part of growth. In a sense, we must do everything at once. There is nothing that can be left undone. And yet, if we keep authenticity as a part of our major concern, any one aspect that we begin with will lead to each of the others.

If somebody asked me where to start in this community-school transformation enterprise, I would say it really wouldn't matter where you started. Any place will do. It is persons that matter. The Buddhist tradition teaches that if one person can be good, the actions of that one person can ripple out to the world. That should not be taken as a simplistic statement. One teacher/ learner in the community who is committed to the discovery and the cherishing of the authentic wherever it is to be met, one person alive to local and well as global reality, one intrepid tester of that reality, can be the lever that moves the entire educational system to a new place.

Mario Fantini

8

FROM SCHOOL SYSTEM
TO EDUCATIONAL SYSTEM

As someone who has worked inside the system of public
schools and, more recently, on the outside, let me try to state my
position regarding the future of American education. First, I am
reasonably optimistic—although I must confess that having heard
Buckminster Fuller, I am about to reassess my optimism a little
bit. According to Buckminster Fuller, humanity may have only
eight to ten years left to control its own unique destiny and to alter
the course of the tragic misuse of resources that has characterized
life in the twentieth century. If this does not occur, civilization will
collapse and after that, nature will take over. Thus, it is now more
than ever important that education have an impact on the future.

In the course of the last century, we have developed a school
system that has steadily moved toward reaching everyone. In 1900
the public schools graduated less than 10 percent of the population,
while by 1970 the figure was closer to 70 to 75 percent. The mission ascribed to this universal system of public schools over the
past decades has been to provide the masses with basic literacy, to
help in the acculturation of our pluralistic population to normative
mainstream values (especially during the great immigration periods),
and to cater to the manpower needs of an industrial, capitalist economy. As such, the schools have attempted to deal with the intellectual development of those learners who were considered "academically able" and who were expected to progress through the schools. At
the same time, alternate streams for those who were perceived to
be not college-bound and thus suitable for earlier vocational training
were created. The structure designed to reach the masses was
mainly developed around the schoolhouse, age-group norms, stan-
dardization in curriculum and construction, courses of study,
specially prepared professional and licensed personnel, and a

pattern of reporting that ranked the learner in relation to others.
In an attempt to keep pace with new societal demands, a secondary
system of add-ons, which included adult education, special education, vocational education, early childhood education, compensatory
education, and so forth, was introduced.

While the school-age population expanded, so did the structure, and the additional resources necessary to approach the tasks
were (relatively speaking) readily available. However, during the
1970s, we have begun to experience the limits of growth in both the
school-age population and in our resources. Our society is undergoing a significant transformation process that is characterized by
such symptoms as intergenerational splits, moral and ethnical decay, economic instability, energy shortages, environmental pollu-
tion, the proliferation of mass weapons of destruction, a population
explosion, global starvation, familial and community deterioration,
and violence. These symptoms point to a society under severe
strain whose needs are clearly beyond the capacity of any one institution, even one so all-encompassing as our school system. What
has long been forecast is coming true: humanity is involved in a
race between education and catastrophe, between merely struggling
for survival and trying to achieve the true fulfillment of human potential. Societal forces seem to control us rather than the other
way around. Through education, however, humanity can hope to re-
gain control over its own fate.

Therefore, if it's not too late, educated people who can begin
to correct the wrongs surrounding us all, who not only care deeply
about the negative conditions that thwart the development of human
beings but also have the competence to act in ameliorative ways,
are vitally needed. Fully educated persons have a disciplined sense
of caring and possess the expertise to perform the major societal
responsibilities because they have learned the political, economic,
and social roles required for constructive problem solving in our
society. Unless we are capable of delivering such quality education
to every citizen, human and societal survival will be in clear and
present danger.

FROM A SCHOOL SYSTEM TO AN
EDUCATIONAL SYSTEM

In my view, the conversion of a free universal school system
to an educational system represents the direction of reform that we
must take in the decades ahead to provide universal quality education. I think that we are very close to declaring that education is no
longer a privilege but a right, and that every citizen should have

the right to a quality education. We have finally begun to approach the view that quality health care should be a citizen's right, and I think that education should not lag too far behind in this quest. In fact, certain states have already passed legislation that is tantamount to the beginning of a definition of the right to a quality education. When the members of a society believe that it is necessary to have quality education as a right, and no longer as a privilege, then a shift in expectations begins to take place. When it was a privilege, children went to the school and if the school setting provided sufficient opportunities for growth, then they were fortunate; if not, they were unfortunate. However, if the American public today believes that quality education is essential for our future success—that it is related to our very survival—then the policy makers will have to deal with it in a different way than they previously have done. This is, in fact, just what is beginning to happen.

Dissatisfied Customers

What we have, really, is the convergence of a pluralistic population with a school system that was never meant to deal with universal literacy, and certainly not meant to educate everyone in the context of today's society. Schooling used to be oriented mainly toward dealing with literacy, civic orientation, and the relationship between the school's and the society's manpower needs. Today, however, people are saying that every child should have a right to be fully educated, to control his or her own destiny, to develop his or her own potential—in short, to be viewed as a distinctive and worthy person. Thus, different objectives are involved in educating today's children. But the model on which our current school system is based is simply not equipped to accomplish these objectives. As a result, we are beginning to see symptoms of the decline of this institution. The expectations are there and the people on the inside are trying very hard to deliver. However, school personnel are shaped by the structure of the system in which they work, and that structure as it currently exists simply does not have the capacity to respond to the enormous societal changes that have occurred in recent years. It is as if the citizens in our society are saying to us something similar to what they said to the scientific community a few years ago. At that time the American public said, "We want to reach the moon. We want to explore space. That should be our new mission." And the scientific community responded, "Yes, we'll develop the model that is appropriate." At this point in time, we need to develop a new _educational_ model.

When I look at certain social indicators today, I see that the resolution of educational issues is increasingly a political phenomenon; the advent of the educational consumer necessitates a clarification of our citizens' rights with regard to the education of their children. In this context, a new mission is evolving. People are beginning to say, "What happens if I feel that my children are not getting a quality education? To whom do I appeal?" The notion of educational malpractice is beginning to surface. Parents, families, and communities are starting to say, "Just a minute. Perhaps we will have to recall this delegation. After all, we created this place, and if 'they' cannot keep pace, then what are our options?"

It is not surprising that we are seeing a rise in citizen awareness and a call for active supervision of what goes on in educational institutions. I was involved in the so-called "school wars" in New York City, where there was an uprising of educational consumers who posed the question, "If these are public schools, to whom do they belong and to whom should they be held accountable? And what happens if we believe, as recipients of a service, that we are not getting the quality education that we think we need, especially today when quality education is essential to our future as a nation?" There have been instances of communities reclaiming their schools in an attempt to say that, at least in the public sector, citizens should be able to clarify the goals and objectives of the school system for themselves. As such, we as citizens delegate to specialists the responsibility for implementation, and we reserve for ourselves the role of accountant. If Johnny can't read, or if Johnny's talents haven't been developed, and if that is what we expected as our goal, then we have a right to an assessment. We are witnessing the advent of legislation that has as its goal the return of authority through economic means to the learner, as a way of building a new educational system. Innovations such as what is called the "voucher plan," which in essence shifts authority back to the family, are also growing in number. Ideally, the family should have the authority to pick and choose—all the way from saying "I'm going to do it all," to saying "I'm going to select from certain kinds of schools," to saying "I'm satisfied with the status quo."

Currently, in my estimation, anywhere from 30 to 40 percent of the people who use the public schools (where 85 percent of Americans send their children) are dissatisfied with the services they are receiving. Thus, a critical mass of discontented customers exists today. And I think that these individuals will increasingly come to constitute a political force, and that educational reform will be played out in legislative chambers and in judicial halls to an even greater extent than it is right now. If 60 percent of the people are satisfied with the service they are getting, then they have the right

to leave things as they are. But a significant 40 percent are clearly
requesting something else. The question of how we can deal with
this remains. How do we keep the best of the current system while
we move forward to update it? How can we protect the rights of citizens in our pluralistic society? Do we say that, since 60 percent is
a majority, then what's good enough for the 60 percent is good enough
for everybody? Or, is it possible to work toward satisfying a variety
of interests?

More specifically, how do we respond to the perception, which
is growing, that we have expected the schools to accomplish too
much? While we were in a period of seemingly unlimited growth,
when resources were plentiful, we kept building the current, many-
layered structure to satisfy the changing needs of society. Now this
structure seems outmoded, unwieldy, and duplicative. The debate
over its appropriateness is becoming divisive and increasingly political. The interested parties are coming together. However, whereas
historically parents and teachers as well as schools and communities
were allies, now they are increasingly involved in confrontations.
They seem to have separate and conflicting agendas. Thus, the fac-
tions involved are organizing themselves to compete in the political
arena over the means and ends of delivering a comprehensive education. Increasingly this divisive atmosphere becomes a counter-
productive environment for the next generation. The question is,
how do we make our way out of such an arena of power politics?

New Structures and Functions

I have already outlined the reasons why a postindustrial, democratic society such as ours requires an educated citizenry in order
to survive and prosper. Therefore, in order to accomplish this
goal, a comprehensive educational system must replace the comprehensive school system that currently exists and which is still rooted
to the needs of the past. We need a structure capable of coping with
the future. This transformation will necessitate not only a redefini-
tion of function and delivery methods, but a realignment of the basic
interested parties: the recipients of educational services (parents
and students, other taxpayers) and the deliverers of these services
(professional educators, other community units, including business
and industry, labor, government, and the cultural and scientific
agencies).

In today's world, the old ways of updating our schools through
add-ons, appendages, and remediation are no longer appropriate.
Our present school system has not only spread itself thin, but has
developed unnecessary duplication. As society has become more

complex, it has delegated increased responsibility to the schools—responsibility that the system is not equipped to handle. We therefore need to convert our school system into an educational system. To accomplish this goal, a much broader conception of resource utilization will have to be considered. The new educational system should systematically link a complex of institutions and agencies. The schools should be linked to a strengthened family, to multicultural neighborhoods, and to cultural, scientific, and recreational agencies in the communities.

In one sense, we are at the point of asking each agency to perform certain functions contributing to a comprehensive educational system, thereby returning to first principles of social organization. In short, we are returning to a structure in which the family and parents are expected to perform certain "key" educational responsibilities—perhaps today with the help of newly developed parenting support opportunities that are appropriate to the kind of diverse society we now have. Through their updated resources, the business and arts communities can be asked where talents can be identified and developed. Similarly, spiritual leaders can join in providing sensitive formats for the development of moral and ethical attitudes that enhance the noblest values of a free and just society. The considerable power of the mass media can be utilized to reach all learners on a number of crucial issues that affect our lives. This will enable the performers who have entertained and inspired us in the past to use their appeal for more serious educational ends.

Within the confines of the schoolhouse, schools could never accomplish all this. Expecting them to do it alone is to continue on a path that can only lead to greater frustration for all concerned. Clearly we have learned that the quality of life in our great metropolitan areas cannot be developed, or even maintained, without excellent education. Yet the overburdening of the schoolhouse has had a destructive effect. It is time to utilize the rich learning environments and talents in the cities themselves through a new and more dynamic linkage of the schools to the other educational units affecting the growth of each person. Therefore, just as in earlier times when the schools, the family, and the churches shared the responsibilities for learning and teaching, so will it be under the educational system of the future. But these fundamental units will be joined by other agencies such as business and industry, human services and government, to form a new educational network—all under the coordination of primary development specialists, educators, and boards of education.

As our school-age population levels off, the current and future restrictions we face in the direct allocation of resources to the schools necessitate a search for new priorities and resources. We now appear to be in the initial stages of transforming our school system into an educational system. The first phase of this transformation will be accomplished through diversification of our delivery of educational services. In the past, the 15 percent who have used private schools—the people who could afford it, the people who felt strongly about it—have always had options. They could go to a prep school, an academy, a Montessori school, a spiritual school, a military school. But the great majority who went into the public sector, because of their sheer numbers, have received a rather standardized approach. The public schools are, ever so slowly, beginning to take a lesson from the private schools and initiating efforts of diversification. This has also taken the form of more options—all the way from liberating styles of teaching and trying to find a more fruitful match between styles of teaching and styles of learning, to introducing different kinds of classrooms from those that have traditionally existed, to forming schools within schools as well as separate schools.

One other important development that has arisen in this transformation process concerns the orchestration of multiple resources within and outside of the schools. We are on the way to becoming a society that relies not only on school-based services but on community-based services that include schools. Linking the schools to the business and industrial environments for talent development, to the health agencies for nutritional awareness and drug education, to insurance companies for driver training, to the arts community for cultural and aesthetic literacy, and to spiritual leaders for moral and ethical growth are but a few of the activities that need to be coordinated. Such expertise can be delivered by a reformed educational system and under the direction and supervision of educators who continue to be accountable to the public for promoting the growth of each learner.

An important consideration in the coordination and interlinking of these resources, talents, and tasks is their cost-effective potential. Surely it is conceivable that the many billions of dollars spent by business and industry on their own training systems and the millions of dollars spent by our libraries, museums, and cultural agencies on life-long learning opportunities could be harnessed in such a way as to avoid unnecessary duplication and to help coordinate and reorganize educational services so as to provide a fuller and more comprehensive utilization of existing resources. In addition, public policy can facilitate cooperation among these institutions through various incentive and tax benefit plans. The overall goal is to provide a comprehensive educational system based on optional paths to quality education for each person. No one agency is capable of being all things to all people, but a systematic orchestration of resources, beginning with the school and extending into the community, may bring us closer to accomplishing our most cherished educational ideals.

THE QUESTION OF LEADERSHIP

For me, the fundamental problem with such a monumental reform of the system is, who will be held accountable? Who are the coordinators? Who are the people who guide the transformation of a school system to an educational system? Should the school system become the major umbrella under which all the resources that will go into an educational system should be gathered? Or— given declining enrollments and the change in its original mission, as well as the existence of time-tested methods for teaching certain basic knowledge—should we allow the current <u>school</u> system to become one small subset of an educational system, but not expect the leadership to come from that quarter? Instead, we could get people from business and industry, from cultural communities, and from all other quarters that could be readily tapped to form an <u>educational</u> system, and begin to conceptualize a whole new structure.

The challenge, it seems to me, is what the role of the educator should be during this period. My bias is that I would like to be able to convert the structure that we have—to update the institution that we have created in such a way that it could become the umbrella for the new, coordinated educational system. I am going to assume that the majority of educators who have devoted themselves to growth and development would, through some revitalization, be willing and eager to recommit themselves unswervingly to the best interests of the learner—regardless of age, background, sex, or race—because of the ample promise a new educational system can offer. As such, they should come forward as the chief accountability officers, the ones to be held responsible for the reform of the old system. The new system that will come to the fore, whether we are part of it or not, will have a major impact not only on our daily lives but on the kind of society we develop. Education will become the means by which people renew themselves, and by which society is renewed.

Now, it is one thing to say that we could transfer responsibilities to the business or arts communities for career or talent development, and so forth. But a series of questions always come to mind:

1. Would shifting responsibility necessarily create a sound educational environment?
2. Is what's good for General Motors necessarily what's best for the learner?

So I think that the public will want to look to some group for asumption of the responsibility for assuring that whatever we do serves the interests of the learner. Here is where I think the major role of those of us who are in professional schools of education lies. So my challenge to you is this: given the fact that most of us are, when the bell rings, going back into a structure that controls our behavior to a large degree, can we rise to that occasion? Can we conceptualize an environment that doesn't yet exist? Can we enter sensitively, and tap the political and economic sources of power that will provide the major locomotion for our transition from a school system to an educational system?

Hazel Henderson

9

THE POLITICS OF
RECONCEPTUALIZATION

I must begin by admitting that I know very little about academically based education, and even less about theories of education. I did not go to college, and I can only speak from my personal life experience—which must be what leads me to believe that we need to trust our own experience more and that the most effective education is often experiential. Unfortunately, academic education (what little of it I see as a guest lecturer at universities around this country) too often has become analogous to a process in which we teach people how to ride bicycles by allowing them to read about riding bicycles, to make models on the blackboard about riding bicycles, and to analyze the parts of the bicycles. But the one thing we never allow people to do is to get on the bicycle and experience learning to ride it by falling off a few times.

"TRUTH IN EDUCATION"

In seeing effective education as experiential, I share a perspective with Doris Lessing, with whom I feel some affinity. She's also British, and she left school when she was 14. I left school when I was 16. She says, in the introduction to her book The Golden Notebook, "The talents every child has, regardless of official I.Q., could stay with them throughout life if they were not regarded as commodities with a value in the success stakes. We are taught from the start to distrust our own judgment, submission to authority, how to search for other people's opinions, how to be critics and reviewers, never original or imaginative judgers." She says that she felt very "psyched out" at having to quit school at 14, and then in retrospect she realized that she felt lucky—that she'd not missed out

119

on something, but instead had gained something more valuable. I share that feeling. Doris Lessing also said that "If young people going into educational situations were read a sort of 'truth in education disclaimer,' it might be a useful thing." And this was her suggestion for a "truth in education disclaimer":

> You are in the process of being indoctrinated. We have not yet evolved a system of education that is not a system of indoctrination. We are sorry, but this is the best we can do. What you are being taught here is an amalgam of current prejudice and the choices of this particular culture. The slightest look at history will show how impermanent these must be. You are being taught by people who have been able to accommodate themselves to a regime of thought laid down by their predecessors. It is a self-perpetuating system. Those of you who are more robust and individual than others will be encouraged to leave and find ways of educating yourself and educating your own judgment. Those that stay must remember always that they are being molded and patterned to fit into the narrow and particular needs of this particular society.

What I would add is that this particular society, and all other mature, late-stage, industrial societies like it, is now changing very drastically. These societies are undergoing a profound socioeconomic transition which is still so little understood that it's referred to in rearview mirror terms such as "postindustrial" state. We are, in essence, backing into the future while looking into the rearview mirror.

The transition metaphor is now being used by most futurists, but the question of what this transition is remains rather unsure. There are many ways of looking at the transition. One way that is very meaningful for me is that it is a transition from the Petroleum Age to the Solar Age: from the economics of maximizing production, consumption, and waste based on nonrenewable resources to an economics based on renewable resources managed for sustained-yield productivity. I proceed under the assumption that the logic of the industrial era (utilitarianism, materialism, positivism, reductionism, instrumental rationality, and the Cartesian world view) is now exhausted. I see the "Yang" emphasis of this Cartesian industrial era that we're leaving now transforming itself into a new expression of what I like to call "Yin" modes—more subjective, more intuitive, more spontaneous, and more ideational.

My favorite metaphors for this transformation are organic and ecological. For example, the cycles of entropy and syntropy that go on all the time on this planet: the composting of old cultures providing for the birth of the new, as described in the writings of such people as Georgescu-Roegen, who has written the last word, I think, in economic reconceptualizing in his The Entropy Law and the Economic Process (1971). Karl Polanyi's book The Great Transformation, which was written in 1944, is also a marvelous way to look at our era today. And I recently rediscovered the marvelous volumes that Pitirim Sorokin wrote between 1937 and 1941, Social and Cultural Dynamics. He sees, in the last chapter of Social and Cultural Dynamics, the Twilight of Sensate Culture. "Sensate" in his terminology means an empirical culture where all things are valued and validated only by our external senses and only the quantifiable is real. Sorokin understood, in that last chapter, exactly what's happening today, and that makes it a very exciting book to reread.

So, we are awakening from our technological trance—what William Blake called "Newton's Sleep." There are signs of a cultural transition in the emergence of an abundance of Cartesian intellectual schematization: the rococo proliferation of disciplines, models and algorithms; of fanciful math, fanciful geometry, fanciful physics, and all of the baroque elaboration of empty technique. I think that this compulsive schematization, if viewed honestly, is what the business world might call "intellectual product differentiation." The number of variables a scholar has in her theoretical model has become not just a new form of scholasticism but, in effect, a new competitive marketing tool for intellectual mercenaries. We also see a transition in the proliferating paradoxes all around us in our culture, which are a sign of the breakdowns of our existing cultural paradigms: after all, paradoxes are only complementarities if you view them from the larger system perspective.

Traditional, and most existing academic institutions were devised to transmit the culture of industrialism and the values of the now waning Petroleum Age. Now those institutions are caught in a severe lag. They're still a virtual Tower of Babel bogged down in all of those curious compartments called disciplines—as if reality were really carved up into pieces marked economics, geography, math, and physics. Our present-day academic institutions may, I believe, increasingly become warehouses for the intellectual paraphernalia of the industrial, rationalistic, Cartesian era of the past 300 years, just as our museums became the repositories for much of the earlier medieval culture, the era of faith. We shall certainly need to conserve the knowledge generated during the Cartesian, industrial period which is now ending, and all of it should be sifted and composted, repatterned, reconceptualized, and eventually recycled into the new culture. But I think that many of its fragments will be of little use in dealing with the transition that our culture must undergo at this point if it is to survive.

BACK TO BASICS

I am talking, here, about the transition to the Solar Age and to planetary culture. If we're going to recycle our culture and recycle ourselves—and that will be the requirement, I believe, for a successful transition—then we are going to need to go back to basics. Of course, many academics and educators are groping in this direction. I hear some of the signals coming from various academic debates, but all too often the academic discussions about what back-to-the-basics means also seem to take place within the traditional educational paradigm—namely, the "basics" are reading, writing, and arithmetic. But I don't mean that sort of back-to-the-basics at all, and, in any case, academic institutions are now too over-grown and too top-heavy to even address simple educational agendas. They already have such a heavy investment in tenured faculty, buildings, hierarchical structures, and construction programs that they could never deliver really simple, basic education with such an enormous overhead.

So, I suggest that we must _really_ go back to basics. I would start, for example, with a first question: "Where are we in time and space?" All our crises are conceptual crises. In many ways, we humans on this planet are like a colony of termites that has, for all of its generations, lived in the beam in the basement of an old house, and we have developed termite geography, termite mathematics, and termite physics. Finally, in this generation, we have broken through the confines of that beam and suddenly we find that not only are we in a beam in a house, but that the walls are falling down, the roof has blown off, and we are confronting an enormous new vista. Obviously, we have to create a new math, a new geography, a new physics, and a new _everything_ to map this new space-time context. Futurism must be, most essentially, such a change in perspective. The loveliest example of the kind of change in perspective that futurism entails is in the motto of the Values Party, a new political party in New Zealand, that embodies many of our futurist ideas and says, "We do not inherit the world from our parents, we borrow it from our children." That's the sort of change of perspective that I think futurism involves.

All of our _conceptual_ crises are rooted in _perceptual_ crises and so the task is going to be to reperceive everything around us. To do that, we're going to have to use _all_ of our faculties, not just our eyes and our minds and our left brain hemispheres; not just the linear, sequential, reductionist learning enterprise that we've been involved in; and not just the sex role polarization that has gone along with that way of perceiving the world. To achieve the transition, we are going to have to reorchestrate all of our senses and we are going to have to study the resulting whole new system as whole selves, because you can't study whole systems unless you are a whole self. We're going to have to study the new situations we have created with our bodies, our minds, our left and right brains, our emotions, our intuitions; and we're going to have to develop systemic awareness. We're going to have to develop androgynous consciousness and reawaken from the Cartesian trance that we have been in. We're going to have to learn through the pores of our skin; we're going to have to tap into the information that's locked in our muscles and in our organs.

The second question we have to address in the back-to-the-basics curriculum is, "Who are we?" Are we protoplasmic creatures molded by our former conditioning? Are we naked apes? Are we "Homo economicus," as the economists would have us believe? Are we evolutionary beings? Are we transcendent co-creators? Are we gods? Any good back-to-the-basics approach is going to have to begin with such fundamental questions. We're also going to have to teach/learn (two sides of the same coin) the ability to see with new vision—as if we were extraterrestrials. We will have to be able to imagine that we are extraterrestrials, approaching this planet for the first time and meeting these strange creatures, Homo sapiens. Only when we see ourselves as extraterrestrials will we be able to create the necessary perspective and develop the necessary sense of the absurd so that we can see the convoluted knots of cultural fabric in which we have become enmeshed.

Back-to-the-basics requires that we see how humans envision themselves. We need to understand, for example, how we metabolize and how we excrete in our dwellings, in our communities, and in our cities. The basic texts for this will not be found in libraries under "architecture," "urban affairs," or "city planning." We're going to need to use our own bodies as the metaphors for exploring our surroundings. More likely texts will include such simple tracts as The Toilet Papers by Sim Van der Ryn (1978) who was the founder of the Farrallonet Institute of Alternative Technology in California. The foreword to this book was written by the rural poet, Wendell Berry, and it starts like this:

Obviously The Toilet Papers is about how we excrete.
It's about shit. If I urinated and defecated into a pitcher
of drinking water and then proceeded to quench my thirst
from the pitcher I would undoubtedly be considered

crazy. If I invented an expensive technology to put my
urine and feces into my drinking water, and then invented another expensive and undependable technology
to make the same water fit to drink, I might be thought
even crazier. It is not inconceivable that some psy-
chiatrists would ask me knowingly why I wanted to
mess up my drinking water in the first place. But our
present "sane" solution to the problem of excretion is
to have me urinate and defecate into a flushed toilet,
from which the waste is carried through an expensive
sewerage works which supposedly "treats" it and pours
it into the river from which the town downstream pumps
it, purifies it, and uses it for its drinking water. Thus,
private madness, through a great deal of expense and
engineering becomes public sanity. This is permitted
by our habitual disregard of consequences: we live by
buying and selling the causes of every conceivable
blight from cancer to famine, and then are continually
astonished to find that these causes have their inevit-
able effects. As a society, we never look ahead of us,
at the generations that will follow, and at the impedi-
ments we are throwing in their way.

My point is that we are going to have to start at the very beginning with a proper sense of humility, and if we do that we will
discover, to our amazement, that we have to begin by studying our
own excrement—relearning what it is and relearning its proper role
in human affairs and in the biosphere. Next, we have to study the
sun because we've forgotten about the sun—what the sun is to us and
to our planet. It's our Mother Star. Even the most so-called "primitive" peoples knew that. I'm always amused if people ask me, when
I'm talking about alternative energy, "Well, how much of my house
could really be heated by solar energy—what percentage?" And I always have to say, "Well, if the sun weren't preheating your house it
would be several hundred degrees below zero." People just have
forgotten about the sun. So we have to learn again about the sun.
We have to study plants and all other life forms, and relearn our
relationship to them and our dependence on them. After all, they
created us as their waste disposal units. We have to pull back the
many veils that we have woven to intermediate between us and all of
these primary realities: our technologies (hardware and software),
our cities, our buildings, our paradigms, our disciplines, our drugs,
all of our thought forms and their manifestations that comprise the
technological furniture of our age. This proliferation of technological furniture and artifacts now preempts our social imagination and

our individual creative responses. It colonizes our brains with instant and inappropriate answers to questions we haven't even framed or asked. Then we must learn to read our technological furniture with awareness of its meanings and purposes so as to judge whether or not it leads us in directions that we really want to pursue.

ALTERNATIVES

After all, there are many different kinds of technology: "machismo" technologies, Yang technologies, the death-oriented technologies of Thanatos. There are the technologies of Eros developed out of love and life, which are technologies for understanding and for human awareness, which can help develop ecological harmony. We must explore our motivation in the search for knowledge; do we learn out of the fear of death, or do we learn out of the motivation of love, for play, for curiosity, desire for empathy, and communion with creation? These are the more benign motives for knowledge that we've almost forgotten. The new learning/teaching agenda must be concerned with reframing these newest/oldest questions.

Of course, in no society would one expect the dominant culture to produce such basic questions, or to provide cadres of questioners. Questions do not arise out of complacency and comfort, so we have to look to the out groups for questioners. As the dominant forces, groups, and institutions of our declining industrial culture begin to lose their ability to govern and to manage events, and as their pronouncements begin to lose their explanatory power, they are creating a cadre of dissidents, which is our cultural opportunity. For example, today's leaders tell us that we must consume our way back to prosperity, while at the same time they tell us that we have a materials and energy shortage. Even these cognitive dissonances are useful in that they spur some of us to question the basic assumptions of our culture. Alternative patterns of action, organization, behavior, perception, and theorizing thus are generated in society's out groups or in repressed populations, whether they happen to be women, or blacks, or Indians, or children, or Chicanos, or the "cranks," or the off-beat, or the eco-freaks, or even the insane as Ronald W. Laing, Thomas Szaz, and others have so eloquently described.

This, I think, is the meaning of the recent boom in alternative movements of all kinds, and of the creation of new definitions and cultural expressions, and of the restructuring of language and knowledge that characterizes all social revolutions, including today's citizen movements, whether they're movements for peace, or economic justice, or racial and sexual equality, or environmental or consumer protection, or alternative technology, or alternative energy, or alternative education. Citizen movements are spontaneous social feedback mechanisms that alert the public about overlooked anomalies and problems not accounted for in the traditional formulations. They're like pain alerting the body to its dysfunctions. Citizen movements are also an incredibly efficient educational mechanism. They're not hierarchical but they focus on teaching/learning with a mutual and simultaneous model of education: the "each one teach one" model. They're also the kind of experiential modes of learning that Kurt Lewin described as "action research"—hypothesizing, then validating in the real sociopolitical world. Citizen movements also enable everyone to advance at their own pace and to design their own curriculum of issues to suit their own needs, emotional states, and motivations.

The most efficient adult education is being done by these citizen groups, and focuses not only on domestic and community issues, but also on global issues—whether it's the hunger action groups; or the groups investigating corporate accountability such as the one I'm proud to be associated with (The Council on Economic Priorities in New York), where we assess the social performance of corporations rather than their economic performance; or the anti-nuclear proliferation groups; or the new political parties like the one I mentioned in New Zealand (The Values Party). The Values Party, for example, which won 6 percent of the vote in the last election in New Zealand, based its whole platform on the rejection of the values of both dominant parties—the money culture, the success culture. Their specific agenda was to create a triangulation point: to pull politics out of that sterile axis where both parties sounded the same and where both parties wanted to maximize GNP as the measure of all things.

The new curriculum subjects revolve around such major social issues, not around "disciplines" like economics, sociology, or even future studies. The planet is the programmed learning environment, and the curriculum subjects include the following: nuclear proliferation—learning about the technological extensions of ourselves and about how we lost control of them; cancer—a karmic lesson in correcting our relationship with the biosphere; inflation—a lesson in correcting our relationships with each other. Yet another curriculum subject is the global interdependence we have created with our globe-girdling technological hardware. We have, in fact, created an interdependent planet whether we like it or not. And that world is now going to teach us that ethics can only begin with a recognition of that interdependence.

With our culture so clearly on the verge of a major transformation, a very basic question is how do we avoid total breakdown and achieve instead a breakthrough? Because whenever a culture loses its coherence (as ours clearly has) there is a moment of enormous opportunity to redefine everything that is going on. Yes, it can be a breakdown, but it also can be a breakthrough to a new form. Amazingly, much of the educational work searching for answers to this question is being carried on by citizen groups: The Schools of Living, for example, that were started after the Depression by Ralph Borsodi. In these schools—of which about 55 remain— the curriculum focuses on re-integrating people's lives, and understanding the primary relationships between shelter and provisioning and how they relate to the macro-culture that we have created. The Schools for Living are still here, all over this country, quietly educating people in a way that can help achieve a breakthrough instead of a cultural breakdown. Equally educational are the projects started by people like Matt Taylor in Kansas City. Matt is rehabilitating a whole neighborhood of Kansas City, bringing together young unemployed people in the inner city and teaching them to rehabilitate houses; teaching them construction skills and paying them with shares in his corporation, called the Renascence Corporation, which is a collective. They have now reached a critical mass and are growing so fast that they're able to acquire a new house and rehabilitate it almost every six months. In fact, they're now creating libraries and study centers, and citizens are literally learning to rehabilitate their society.

Similarly, there is the work that James Robertson started in Britain with a group called "Turning Point." Robertson has just written an excellent new book, called The Sane Alternative, in which he articulates what he calls the "SHE Future." He has five different scenarios of possible futures—two of which are the "HE Future" and the "SHE Future." The "HE Future" is the Hyper-Exponential one: the Herman Kahn vision of expanding onward and upward, culminating in space colonies—the last play of the "progress ethic." But the "SHE Future" is the one Robertson calls the "Sane, Humanistic, Ecological Future," and so Turning Point members are setting up citizens' study groups in Britain around these ideas.

Another educational activity conducted by citizens groups was Sun Day—May 3, 1978. The Sun Day was coordinated as a new organizational model that I think is a promising one for the future: it is an organic organizational model, a "Brush Fire" model. All that was done centrally in Washington with a small office was to broadcast the idea—Celebrate the Sun, any way and anywhere you want to on this planet! And Sun Day groups organized themselves in about 35 or 40 different countries. They all did whatever they wanted:

dances, festivals, parades, and so forth. The basic idea was simply to encourage people to do whatever they wanted on May 3, and then to have them tell us about it so that we could focus media attention on it. That's the "Brush Fire" model of organization—a nonhierarchical networking of autonomous human beings that share the same consciousness of where the world is.

DIMENSIONS

What I'm saying is that there's no way to be an educated human being in our interdependent, industrial society without some involvement in social action/research. It is, after all, impossible to be human without some sort of political dimension. After you've got it together in your own life and you've worked out good interpersonal relationships, and you are pursuing a "right livelihood," the important question is, then what? What do you do after your tenth weekend encounter group? Then what? It seems that after you've got it together in your head, then you have to move out. And new personal visions must lead to new actions and to new politics. Now, I don't mean the old geographical politics that goes on in that eighteenth-century institution called the United States Congress. What I mean is issue politics and "politics by other means"—politics at the annual meetings of corporations, media politics, guerilla theater, social action/research, and consciousness-raising.

Perhaps citizen participation projects are, in fact, a form of existential art. I know such efforts rely on image making, on visualizations of desirable future scenarios, and their communication on intellectual, emotional, and experiential levels all at once. It's rather like painting a moving picture on an undulating canvas or surfing the waves of daily events. I think that while working on Sun Day I realized for the first time that artists were indispensable to the kind of politics I'm talking about. We couldn't, for example, get started with Sun Day until artists made some gorgeous posters of what we were trying to portray—a new/old relationship of remembering about the Sun.

Of course, all of our human doing is partial and compromised because we're only using the material distillation of our infinite selves. We can vaguely remember the perfection of the whole, but our actions involve intersecting the present time to create a specific event which is, of course, always a pale imitation of our visions. In the same way, perception occurs only from a specific vantage point in space and time. In fact, this differentiation may well be the "fall" of which the Bible speaks. For the same reasons, planning is always a delusion: impossible, because any photo of the future must be static. Even if it accurately mapped a specific set of possibilities or probabilities at any point in time, the picture must lose resolution each day as reality goes on its merry way. I know that many are appalled at the array of new uncertainties that we're facing, but I see the happier side of chance: that all could change for the better in the twinkling of an eye. In other words, "randomness" is only a measure of human ignorance.

The hologram has always been a key metaphor for me. Holograms are three-dimensional "pictures" where, even if some part of the image is destroyed, what's left recapitulates the whole. There are, for example, the interpersonal human transactions that are encoded in the ancient wisdom, "do as you would be done by." That's a hologram, a three-dimensional dance at the interpersonal level. Or there's a social hologram—a growing consciousness, building empathy with other groups, the closure of the technologically created rifts between cause and effect. And there's the political hologram—a harmonizing of values, national and international efforts that are moving toward goals clarification: world order models and the building networks of interplanetary consciousness.

All the great spiritual leaders of history were the real futurists, but we have never understood their time frame. In such a context, the planet is the real Skinner-box: our programmed learning environment with all the positive and negative reinforcers to help each of us understand its operating principles: sharing, cooperation, honesty, and love. That's really what the planet is teaching. We'll learn or else we'll be destroyed in the process. And yet the effort to evolve a higher set of ethics and values will not be left to us alone. The planet is gently nudging us along with all of those reinforcers moving us whether we like it or not. And when planetary awareness operates to program and harmonize the actions of all humans, the anarchist's dreams will be realized: voluntary self-restraint of behavior based on the empathy that's possible when each human bit in the hologram recapituates the whole picture.

Dwight W. Allen

10

URBAN EDUCATION:
HOPE AND PROSPECT

In talking about the hope and prospect of urban education, it is difficult to know where to start, but I'd like to start with an analogy suggested by Arthur Clarke: the analogy of the cliff. He said that humanity started out living in a desert where things were very sparse and life was very difficult. Because things were sparse and life was difficult, man started walking. Pretty soon he came to a very verdant valley where life was much easier. The necessities of life were in greater abundance, and so he multiplied, and the valley became too crowded, so he walked on. Eventually, mankind found himself living in a greenhouse with very intensive cultivation where he could have an even higher standard of life. But, again, he multiplied and things began to be crowded, so he started walking again. After a while he came to a cliff, and on the top of the cliff was the Garden of Eden, but he couldn't reach the garden by walking anymore. He had to do something different. A different process was required. The real question that we face, says the analogy, is how to shed our walking shoes and get some clamp-ons or other kinds of climbing equipment.

To put it another way, we can no longer continue with our more gradual technological expansion. We have a mentality that "more is better." The best way that we have come up with for solving the problems of society is simply to grow—the frontier mentality. Anytime we have a problem we just leave for a new frontier, we go on to a new experience. This is one of the things that has made America the successful country it has been: we have been able to simply grow beyond our problems. Today, unfortunately, I'm afraid we are living in a society where we're going to have to abandon our growth mentality, and without this making us pessimistic, because a growth mentality allows us to avoid solving our problems

and a "crunch mentality" forces us to face issues. In education today, I think we need a "crunch mentality" rather than a growth mentality. I think we face a choice: either a collapse of our affluent
lifestyle or the conservation of a moderately affluent lifestyle. We
are in a time of transition. We are leaving a period of an aristocratic elite and approaching a time of a democratic elite. Isn't that
an interesting contradiction in terms: a democratic elite? The
British have an interesting way of thinking about British education
and American education: British education puts the emphasis on the
cream and leaves the skim milk behind; American education thinks
that you can homogenize everything and get all cream. In many ways,
part of the genius of our country is to try to create a lifestyle for
everyone that surpasses the lifestyle that used to be possible only
for a few. I think that we are experiencing a transition from the
aristocratic elite to a democratic elite. We see this at a physical
level and at a psychological level. The average man on the street
no longer has to drive the people's car—the Volkswagen. He can
aspire to much more than that.

We have left a period of cultural isolation, when our job was
to simply learn the culture in which we found ourselves immersed
by birth, and have entered a time when we have to deal with the
problems of a global village. Multicultural education these days has
a very different meaning than multicultural education had even a generation ago. We have left a time of superstition and we're entering
a time of rationalization, a time of understanding. We've left a time
when we had to be creatures of our environment—had to accept the
environment as it was—for a time when we can shape the environment around us. In fact, we now have the expectation of shaping the
environment around us. We've left a time of blind authority to come
into a time of questioning. We've left a time of fatalism and we're
entering a time of choice—and perhaps that word ought to be written
largest of all: a time of CHOICE. Putting it another way, we've
left a time of real scarcity and we're entering upon a time of artificial scarcity. There is an air of unreality about scarcity when
you find an excess of trained manpower, an excess of raw materials,
an excess of demand, and yet you still have unemployment. That is
artificial scarcity. We are not limited by limitations that are real,
but by the limitations of our own ability to manipulate and distribute
the goods and materials of the world. And that is a very sad circumstance, at least as far as I'm concerned. I could never find any jus-
tification, for example, for flying planes around the world half-empty.
It's a human resource to be used, and we're just not smart enough to
figure out how to use it. It's a good example of artificial scarcity.

One of the speakers of the conference, my friend Mr. Dieuzeide
from UNESCO, said that we think of the future in terms of the year

2000, and he pointed out that more than half of the teachers and administrators who will be teaching and administrating in the year
2000 have already been trained. Not that they are merely already
alive, but they have already been trained. That means that if we
have any great expectations about how education will be different in
the year 2000, we'd better think again. We either have to rethink
our expectations or we'll have to come up with something very, very
different between now and then. In fact, Mr. Dieuzeide pointed out
that those who aspire to be teacher educators today aren't influencing
the year 2000, they're actually influencing the year 2100. The calculations he indulged in were as follows: Anyone that you are now
training as a teacher educator will be active until the year 2020.
These teacher educators that you instruct now will be instructing
teachers until the year 2060, and those teachers will be teaching
students until the year 2100. So, you see, the direct result of
teacher education today is an influence that extends to the year 2100.
Of course, there is another way to put it, and that is that our current influences still go back to 1860. I find that very easy to understand and accept, don't you?

SELECTION OR INCLUSION?

One of the influences that, perhaps, will be most significant
in the coming transition is the change from a concept of education
as a selection device to education as an inclusion device. Nowadays
we start with the premise that we've always had in education: at
every stage along the way we select the people who will go to the
next stage. You still see that in most of the countries of the world
today. By the time children finish primary school, the most able
are selected to go on to secondary school, then the most able are
selected to go on to college, and then the most able are selected to
go beyond that. There's always a selection process, and the issue
is always, how do you select? Here in the School of Education we
decided that we would select students for our doctoral program
along different criteria than normally had been used. Instead of
paying attention to GREs (Graduate Record Exam scores) and grade
point averages, we selected on something called "leadership skills."
But nonetheless, however different the process was, it was still a
selection process. We never made the assumption that everyone
ought to come and get a doctorate.

Education that is premised upon a selection process is very
different from education that is premised on an inclusion process.
With an inclusion process, we would be telling teachers, and most
particularly in the inner cities, "You can't select anyone out. You

have to include everybody." That would be a very different process of-education. Yet education is still very much tied to this selective mentality. Americans have dealt with the selection mentality in very creative ways; since we live in a society where everybody has to be above average, we've figured out a way that everybody can be above average by ten points and still fail. Historically, 60 percent is the lowest failing grade, so you can be ten points above average and still fail—that's a uniquely American solution. But, if we were faced with having an educational system that says you can't select anyone out, we'd have to educate <u>everybody</u>. I don't think that our mentality and our methodology are prepared to deal with that circumstance in education. Just think what would happen, for example, in the inner city if everyone got A's. Everyone's reading well; everyone's writing well; everyone's counting well; everyone's very aesthetically prepared, humanistically prepared, and so on. We would no longer have any way of selecting anyone out at any level of education. Would we know how to act? Would we feel that there is any way we could run a society where we have to say to people, "You are now entering the lottery of medical school. We will draw every 110,000th number, and if you are the lucky person, you go to medical school. If you've lost that lottery, the second prize is engineering school, third prize is law school," and so on. What would happen if we lived in a society where education worked? We would need a completely different mentality for an education of inclusion than we need for an education for selection. The mentality isn't there; that's one of the cliffs we have to climb to get to the Garden of Eden. And it really is a <u>cliff</u>, because it's a totally different kind of a process, not just a gradual transition.

It's very popular these days to talk about life "passages." I think maybe we ought to talk about "educational passages." We are trying to define a way to go about the process of urban education, and it would be nice to know what the goals of that education are. When the School of Education was getting established, we had between 40 and 50 committees meeting on different aspects of the school. The only committee that never made its report at the end of the year was the Committee on Goals. We never did get our goals identified. When I say that I'm going to talk about the goals of urban education, you'd better be very suspicious that I'm going to do this in a way that leaves me lots of room to cop out. I'm going to go back to the popular new international definition called "Basic Human Needs." I think that's as good a starting place as any in talking about the goals of urban education. Then we can talk about those goals in such global terms that everybody will agree. People would agree, for example, that education should be such that it helps people gain and maintain their health. That education ought to help a person with a comfortable environment. That education ought to help provide the basis for constructive human relations. That education ought to make a person productive in an economic and social sense. And that education ought to promote a person's independence. You see, these are goals that everybody can march behind and raise the flag to. Unfortunately, we still haven't said anything yet. Because, unfortunately, these goals are at the level of pious hope rather than being anything that you can start following in a classroom.

We also have the issue of the immediate and long-run implications of these goals. One time, an irate mother came marching into the kindergarten class and wanted to know whether what the kindergarten was teaching would help her child get into college. The kindergarten teacher said, "I'll give you a six-month unconditional guarantee on everything I do." I think that in dealing with immediate and long-term goals, perhaps a word that we need to put into our educational lexicon is "anticipation." We need to train children to be able to anticipate, if you will, their future. And then I would like to suggest another goal of education that isn't usually on the standard list but would be on my standard list—to educate an individual to understand and accept well-established limits. I think that people have to have something to push against, and one of the ways that I think education often fails is that we don't give people any such limits. We don't tell them what the constraints are that they're expected to function within. It is very hard for someone to function if they don't know what the appropriate limits of behavior are—for example, the appropriate limits of productivity. You have to have some way to know when you're done, and education is a bad model for that because no one ever knows when they're done. The only way you ever know that you've come to the end of English 9 is that it's June, because if you finish early you always have to go on to another chapter. There is no body of material that's "ninth grade English"; there's not even a body of material that's algebra. The algebra teacher says, "Last year I got to Chapter 19; this year I got to Chapter 21." Did last year's students get gypped or this year's? We don't have limits anywhere in our society. How do you know, for example, when to get a new car—when they change the design? How do you know when a car is worn out? You don't, because our society is not designed to deal with that. That's part of the destructiveness of planned obsolescence. Rather than any kind of intrinsic notion of what limits ought to be—limits on consumerism, limits on relationships (for example, when is a human relationship a valid relationship and when is it exploitive?)—we have artificial limits. I think more than any place else, this is where our society fails. It fails to help us set limits.

We could, of course, become more metaphysical. We could say that society doesn't help us deal with ultimate purpose. But if you think we have trouble with values, wait until you try "ultimate purpose." I think that by a sort of common agreement, we've decided that schools will not enter the hallowed ground of trying to help an individual find his ultimate purpose. So when I say we need to deal with limits, that's a code word for saying I really would like to deal with ultimate purpose, but don't dare. Perhaps we can figure out some of the limits, because without that, I don't think we can make any progress. For example, is there a reasonable way of setting limits in terms of whether or not children ought to be safe going to the bathroom in school or not? Because, in many high schools today, youngsters do not feel safe going to the bathroom. I was talking with a team of educators in Paterson, N.J., and in one of the high schools there the students were complaining that it was not safe to go to the bathroom in school, so they had to risk accepting a truant cut in order to go home and go to the bathroom. Should there be some way of establishing constructive limits in terms of what people can do in school, like go to the bathroom, and what they can't do in school, like preventing people from going to the bathroom? I think that's a fundamental place to start, and if we can't find that kind of limit, then I suspect that we are not going to be very capable of dealing with other problems in schools.

"GOOD TEACHING"

My topic is "Urban Education: Hope and Prospect," and I'd like to point out that good education in the urban schools is no different from good education anywhere. It's only that in other places children can learn in spite of the system, whereas in urban settings they're more likely to learn only because of the system, or to not learn because of the system. Urban education is about the same as any other education, only its flaws are much more obvious and apparent to everyone. One of the things that continues to frustrate us about education, for example, is the definition of good teaching. If you look at the research on good teaching, it all boils down to the fact that good teachers are good boy scouts or girl scouts: effective teachers are open, empathic, creative, and intelligent persons. As my friend Chris Dede said, "So are effective therapists—open, empathic, creative, and intelligent persons. So is almost anyone else that you'd care to associate with by choice—an open, empathic, creative, and intelligent person." So we really haven't said much when we've said that. Here at the University of Massachusetts we have about 20 different programs in teacher education, all of which start from different premises, and it turns out that you can produce very competent, capable, and productive teachers from any of these premises. You can produce teachers where people have designed 2,000 little boxes of skills to check off, and the teachers come along and check them off. They get to be good teachers. Or you can have the Gestalt type of teacher education, where the premise is that any kind of analysis at all destroys the art of teaching. The teachers are supposed to <u>feel</u> the way it goes, to <u>feel</u> the presence of the class. They respond to the immediacy of the needs of the individuals there. And people who go around trying to do that, and who go off on retreats once a month during their teacher training, somehow come out good teachers. Somehow, they come out to be as good teachers as people who are going around checking off little boxes. Part of what that says is that maybe there are differences in styles and preferences of teachers; and maybe that is legitimate. But part of it says that maybe we are really fooling ourselves about what the processes are that really produce good teachers. Maybe what we really need to go back to is that open, empathic, creative, and intelligent person we started with. But that gets to be a little bit dangerous for a professional educator to say, because if you carry that to its logical conclusion, you wind up without much professional education.

But that's not where I wind up at all, because it seems to me that the issue is not whether or not teaching can be analyzed, but <u>what</u> teaching can be analyzed. There is plenty of evidence—our microteaching research, our technical skills of teaching research, our Clinic to Improve University Teaching—that demonstrates very rigorously that it's easy to produce changes in behavior as a result of very explicit training protocols. It's not a mysterious thing. If you have a teacher who mumbles and is rooted to the floor, you can teach that teacher to be a little more animated and to look up a little bit more, and you can even teach them to use a gesture or two. These things are not mysterious; they can be done. Or, in case you think it's all mere gimmickry, one of the places where I've seen this training used most dramatically was with teachers who were teaching in a multiracial situation. Little black children would come up to white teachers, and little white children would come up to white teachers, and you'd look on the video tape and you'd see a very dramatic difference. A little white child would come up, and the teacher would say, "Yes, Johnny." A little black child would come up, and they'd say, "Yes, Johnny." And you could just <u>see</u> the difference. It was very dramatic. It wasn't that the teachers were being deliberately prejudiced. They just didn't know how to act with little black children. So a microteaching protocol was developed where the white teachers were given the opportunity to

physically deal with black kids on a different level. One of the
specific activities that we trained these teachers to do (it may sound
silly, but it worked) was to run their hands through black kinky hair.
Many of these white teachers had never touched black kinky hair. It
had to be done very carefully so that the dignity of the children
wasn't sacrificed, but after the teachers went through this protocol
we saw dramatic differences in the teachers' behavior with little
white children and little black children. Specific training does not
necessarily deal with just small gimmicks; it can deal with some
very fundamental issues.

But, in the same way, there are many judgmental aspects of
teaching that absolutely defy any kind of categorization: they boil
down to common sense, to a presence, a charisma, a style. I'll
never forget two of the students in my teacher education program
at Stanford, because any time I start getting arrogant about a particular style of teaching, I remember Colonel Holly, a retired Army
colonel teaching math. I went to visit him, and when I walked in the
door he jumped up and gave me a dittoed slip of paper. I had to
write my name, where I was from, and why I was there. Then a
child ushered me to a seat, as he'd been trained to do. I sat down,
and he took the slip up to the colonel. Another child came over
and showed me the book, what page they were on, what they were
doing. Soon the colonel snapped his fingers and people passed
things out, and then he snapped his fingers again and people collected them. The people who were supposed to collect them were
absent, so there were people there who collected the things when
people were absent. It went on like that, and I sat there and I
thought, "I'm in the Army!" But the students loved it and they
learned algebra! It was very hard for me to deal with! It violated
everything that I knew about the way we're supposed to deal with
children; sensitively, in an open and relaxed atmosphere. Here,
the students were jumping around and going through hoops and all
the rest of it. Then there was Ellis French—the only student in the
history of microteaching who foiled the youngsters who were role-
playing in microteaching. We had one who played "Know it all"—
that was a favorite role; and one who played "Couldn't care less."
These youngsters were really trained to harass teachers. We invested a lot in their training—we were dealing with bright, liberal
arts graduates who didn't think they needed to be trained as teachers
and we thought we would humble them a little. We humbled them!
We reduced them to tears, except for Ellis. He was the only exception in the history of microteaching. He came in, stood in front
of these youngsters, and looked at them with his big, brown eyes,
and they melted. They could not play their roles. They just sort
of sat there. And the more softly he spoke, the more attentively

they listened. It violated all the rules. He was soft-spoken, he was about as animated as a dishrag, but somehow he could just look at people with those soulful eyes and they wanted to help. And so, as far as I know, there are children out there somewhere helping Ellis, even today. How do you deal with that as a teacher educator? I don't need much convincing these days that there is something more to teaching than simply a list of skills. I think that we are not very well served as teacher educators if we don't recognize some of the more sophisticated, and less easily categorized, dimensions. Incidentally, one of the factors that consistently turns out to be important for a teacher is a good sense of humor. It doesn't make much difference whether you have an English sense of humor or a French or Italian sense of humor, so long as you have one.

If we're going to improve urban education, then there are really three kinds of things we can improve: the organization, the staff, or the curriculum. In my career as an educator I had my fling at improving the organization. It was called "flexible scheduling," and we went around for ten years flexibly scheduling every-thing. I still believe in it. But it turns out that after you get people flexibly scheduled, which they say they want, they don't know how to use it. It's like the first experiment I ever did with video-tape. The variable we were studying was "Would the use of video-tape im-prove teacher education?" Now isn't that a silly thing to ask? But that was the best we could do. We were the first ones to own a video-tape machine and we were trying to justify it in the budget, so the way we did it was to see if it helped teacher education. Twenty years later, we know that the answer is not <u>whether</u> it helps teacher education, but <u>how</u> do you use it in order to help teacher education? In the same way, flexible scheduling will help education, I am con-vinced. It's just that most people do not know how to use it to help education.

After I finished trying to improve the organization of the school for about ten years, I started trying to do the same with the staff, in what we called "differentiated staffing." Everybody agreed that teachers are not interchangeable parts: some are good, some are bad, and some are indifferent. They also agreed that you're never quite sure how to tell who's good, who's bad, and who's indifferent—which, incidentally, I don't agree with! You <u>can</u> tell who's very, very good and who's very, very bad. You just can't tell very much about the people in between. But because we can't tell much about the people in between, we refuse to act on the ones who are very good and the ones who are very bad. That never made much sense to me. When you can get agreement at the .01 level about the very best teacher in the school and agreement at the .01 level about the worst teacher in the school, it seems to me that you ought to treat those teachers somewhat differently! But because we can't figure out about all the other 98, we don't deal with the ones at the end, and that seems to me to make no sense. In any case, we got nowhere with differentiated staffing, and one of the reasons was that any time you start talking to teachers about selecting some to be better and be paid more, they get pretty upset. It turns out that there's a real second-rate, second-class mentality in the classroom. Notice that I didn't say that there are a lot of second-class people in the classroom. I said there is a second-class mentality, because many of those people with that second-rate mentality are first-rate! They're just locked into that mentality. Any time you start talking about choosing teachers to have high responsibility and to be paid more, everybody thinks it's going to be someone else and not them! It was the same when we did a survey at Stanford among entering freshmen. Ninety-seven percent of the entering freshmen said they were below average for the freshmen class. It's as hard for 97 percent of the freshmen to be below average as it is for everyone in American society to be above average.

Anyway, trying to improve the staff didn't produce much, so then we tried improving the curriculum. The amount of monkeying around with the curriculum that goes on is amazing. People add things, make them interdisciplinary; they do all sorts of things to the curriculum. But after they're all done with it, most people are very comfortable with the three R's. They are even uncomfortable with adding a fourth R, though occasionally people will say that the fourth R is responsibility, and there are some others who say the fourth R is art. If the fourth R as art gives you trouble, then writing should give you trouble as the second R, and arithmetic should give you trouble as the third R, right? As far as that's concerned, human development is just as good as a fourth R as any of the others—the "R" is silent in human development.

CHILDREN

Or maybe we've been wrong, all the way around, to talk about the organization, the staff, and the curriculum as a way of changing schools. Maybe we should have had a completely different focus. Maybe we need to focus not on schools at all, but on children, and try to let the organization, staffing, and curriculum in the school grow from what the children are like. Now I am back all the way to the beginning—the question of education as an inclusion process rather than as a selection process. If you are talking about education as a selection process, you can start with an institution; you can say, "All those who are fit, enter, and those who remain fit may go on for more." You start with the institution, and you change the institution internally, but you still select people who are going to succeed in the institution. But if education is an inclusion process, then you start with the children and you say, "What do I want this child to be able to do? What are the basic human needs?" I want him to be healthy. I want him to be productive. I want him to function as an individual. And then I start designing institutions around the needs of that individual. I think that we're edging up to that when we talk about diagnostic and perspective learning packages. And I think we're edging up to it when we talk about mainstreaming for special education. I think we're edging up to it; but we need to climb the cliff, not simply walk on further. It seems to me that we need to find a different starting point for an education of inclusion that begins with an individual and builds an educational structure around the individual. This is particularly poignant in urban education, so let me give you what I consider to be the most powerful contemporary example of the dead end that we're driving ourselves to. I'm talking about the fact that children in the great cities can't read and write, that they don't do their basic skills very well, and that they're not getting jobs. I maintain that the lack of reading and writing is important, but that these youngsters are not getting jobs is not only because they don't read and write. Let me put it another way: whether they're reading and writing will not make more jobs. If these youngsters were reading and writing you might have a different selection process in terms of who gets jobs, but there wouldn't be more jobs. So those people who call for career education and basic education are leading us down a primrose path, because they're disguising the basic issue—which is that the worst thing that could happen in American education would be for everybody to be educated, because that would expose the dysfunctional nature of the society and expose the fact that we have a cliff to climb. We need to find a way to look at the nature of the social structure that we have and see if there is a way that we can get rid of artificial scarcity. We need to see if we can find a way of utilizing the precious talent that we have, and the resources that we have, to create a different life potential. The problem I have with the preoccupation with basic education is that it's basically a "computer-chip" education. What we're really saying is that we're going to train youngsters to act like machines. There's a real undertone of training children to act like machines in the rhetoric of basic education.

Let me first of all make it quite clear that I am not against anybody reading and writing. I'm against reading and writing being viewed as the goal of education. The goal of education, as I said before, is a productive individual who knows how to be healthy; who

knows how to be independent; who knows how to function in interpersonal relationships. Reading and writing are skills that can
help enhance that goal, and any child that doesn't learn to read and
write is handicapped in achieving that goal. But those skills are a
step along the way, not the objective of education.

We often talk about finding a way so that education can overcome disadvantage at home. We want to use education to close the
gap between fortunate and unfortunate kids, but that is one of the
biggest mistakes that anyone ever invented. Because, when you
stop to think about it, if you had an educational system that was
functioning perfectly, absolutely perfectly, then the difference between the children of good backgrounds and those of bad backgrounds
(however you choose to define that) would be even bigger than it is
now. Because any time you find something that works with the
children of disadvantage, it will work even better with the children
of advantage. Or, even if it works equally well, the children that
start out with advantage are going to keep their advantage. I haven't
found anyone yet who would argue that if we find a brilliant new approach to education, we should keep it away from the advantaged.
So those who talk about education to reduce the gap between the dis-
advantaged and the advantaged don't really understand what they're
talking about. They don't understand society; they don't understand
people; they don't understand the process of education; they don't
understand how the institutions work. But it's fine rhetoric because
who can be against reducing this gap? The real issue is whether we
can find a way that people who come from all different kinds of backgrounds can function in terms of their health, their wealth, their
wisdom, their independence, and their ability to choose. People
are created differently. The question is how can these differences
become sources of distinction rather than sources of discrimination?
How can we create a society where the range of human talent that is
appreciated becomes wider, rather than narrower?

Right now, for example, anyone who gets below an 1100 on a
GRE is thought to be inferior. That's a very strange definition of
inferior, isn't it? If we had an education of inclusion rather than an
education of selection, we would find a way for the whole range of
human talents to be identified, developed, and appreciated. If we
are trying to learn instead of trying to solve our problems by running away from them to a new frontier, we should try to solve our
problems by facing and dealing with them as we find them. Another
way of thinking about it is to eliminate the need for upward mobility.
Nowadays, a father is fulfilled if his son gets out of the coal mine
and doesn't have to work there like he did. The father is fulfilled
because the son does not have to choke on the carcinogenic gas that
the father has to choke on! And that's called upward mobility.

There are some other options, like making coal mining something that people don't have to avoid. One of the ways is not to get computer-chipped people to do the mining, but to get computer chips to do the mining. That's a very real option. One of the things wrong with our system now is that many of the tasks that used to require people no longer require people and that creates unemployment. But we could sit back, relax, and enjoy it. Let's figure out a way for coal miners to have sabbaticals every third year. That might make it more desirable to be a coal miner.

We could look to a new reality where the identity of a person is not defined vocationally. Right now you say, "Who are you?" and the answer is, "I'm a teacher." "I'm a carpenter, that's who I am." "I'm a housewife." A good friend of mine who is a professor at Amherst College really blows people's minds because at cocktail parties they say, "Who are you?" And he says, "Im' a poet." They say, "Oh, where has your poetry been published?" And he says, "It hasn't." Well, that makes cocktail party conversations stop right there, because how do you deal with a poet who's never published his poetry? There is silence, and then, depending on whether he likes them or not, he lets them off the hook. If he doesn't like them, they just sort of sit there stewing in their own juice, because they've created their own dead end. But if he likes them, he says, "But I earn my living teaching physics at Amherst." Why, if you teach physics at Amherst to earn your living, do you have to be called a physicist? Can't you call yourself a poet? It's only to the extent that the psychological identity of an individual can be free from vocation that, it seems to me, we can create different potentials for an education of inclusion rather than an education of selection. In such a society, it doesn't have to be bad to be a coal miner. It doesn't have to be bad to be a ticket taker. You don't have to apologize for the way in which you earn your living.

EXPECTATIONS

I am, you see, calling for a renovation in society that goes way beyond the ability of education to influence. So we're back to the problem of setting limits in education, limits in expectation of what the schools are supposed to do. Now, universities are supposed to be dreaming new dreams about society, and I wouldn't want that to stop. But I think that schools have an obligation, at all levels, to teach people how to live in the world in which they find themselves, as well as to dream about the Garden of Eden at the top of the cliff. You need to prepare people to deal with the immediate reality down here at the bottom of the cliff, where it's getting pretty crowded and a little bit steamy. We need to give them everything we can to climb the cliff, and we need to give them the dream of the top of the cliff, so that they have the incentive to climb. And that's the balance which, it seems to me, we have to find. If we are going to create hope in urban education, we don't fool youngsters about the steamy nature of the environment that they are facing now, we don't give them any illusions about immediate access to the Garden of Eden, but we do give them some climbing shoes. We help them find realistic options within the environment in which they find themselves.

I'd like to conclude by focusing on two important words for education: the first one is "moderation," the second one is "ambiguity." It seems to me that we are well served as educators if we learn the principle of moderation; if we learn, and help children to understand, that almost anything that is done to excess becomes bad. Civilization taken to excess becomes bad. Materialism taken to excess becomes bad. Education taken to excess becomes bad. As I said earlier, for example, I think that we have a choice in the immediate future between the collapse of an affluent life style and the moderation of an affluent life style. One of the real problems we have in terms of the energy "crunch" is that we're pretty primitive in terms of the way we deal with energy. The major vehicle for storing energy is the storage battery and one of the ways of thinking about a battery is that a battery will store about 100 Btu's of energy per pound. Now if you want to know how bad that is, you can store 25 Btu (British thermal units) in a pound of rubber bands. You see how primitive we are—our major technology for storing energy is only four times as effective as rubber bands. As you go on, it gets better, because steam will store 1,000 Btu per pound, but it takes lots of pounds to control and contain steam. The nirvana, the Garden of Eden at the top of the cliff, is a pound of hydrogen, through the power produced by fusion, which will produce 260 billion Btu. Now you're starting to talk about something. When you're talking about 100 for a battery or 25 for rubber bands, you really haven't done much yet. So we have a long way to go. We can see that power by fusion would give us this Garden of Eden with an unlimited potential of power, but in the meantime we're still back winding our rubber bands. The moderation with which we use the energy resources we now have will allow us the luxury, if you will, of getting organized for the climb. But, if we waste profligately the energy resources we have now, we'll never make it to the top before we have a collapse in life style, and then we'll have to start from a very much more rugged base.

These are the kinds of choices we face, and I think we are not very good at helping children face them. Recently we did a survey in the Paterson, New Jersey schools, where the students said it was more important for them to study the future than any other subject in the curriculum. Of course, they don't study the future. If we are going to be responsive to needs, we ought to figure out a way to help them study the future. We're back here, trying to create a way to get people their hiking and climbing shoes. Moderation is an extremely important principle in a time of transition, because in a time of transition you tend to swing wildly from excess to excess. So any time you see yourself enthusiastically running after something new, remember moderation.

And then there's that second word, "ambiguity." Somehow, I think educators display an unreasonable arrogance of presuming that they should know. We live in a time of great ambiguity. We're facing that cliff. We've never climbed that cliff before. We're not sure what we need to climb that cliff. And any educator who doesn't feel immersed in this atmosphere of ambiguity, I think, is unreasonably arrogant. I don't care whether you are a "three R's" type, or a "humanistic education" type, or what your particular "bag" is as an educator. I think it's arrogant to assume that you know how to climb that cliff. I think we need to be a bit more humble in our sense of ambiguity. I think we need to be a little more humble in the way in which we help children face an uncertain future. I think we need to be a little more humble in recognizing that it is the nature of man to be imperfect, and that it is the nature of society to be imperfect, and that to deal with this imperfection is perhaps the most important talent we have to transmit to our children. Somehow if we get all that put together; if we find a way to get beyond the little agreement we have on the present of education, let alone trying to figure out and get an agreement on what the future of education ought to be; if we can find a way to get rid of the computer-chip mentality—training children to be machines, and instead train machines to do the job of machines, then in that process we will discover, perhaps, what is essentially human. In the process of doing that, we can give the children who are immersed in an urban setting—which doesn't have limits, which doesn't have a sense of direction, which doesn't have, somehow, a sense of hope—a sense of limits, a sense of direction, and, most important of all, a sense of hope.

Peter H. Wagschal

11

THE FUTURE OF
AMERICAN EDUCATION

INTRODUCTION

I would like, in this brief essay, to speculate both on what I see as the most likely possibilities for American education and on what I see as the most desirable ones. The careful futurist, of course, avoids making this separation, thereby allowing herself the freedom to make a good future happen by the act of will. No doubt I, too, will succumb to that temptation from time to time, but I will try to avoid the more blatant examples of it—like when Westinghouse informs us that the demand for electricity in the next 30 years will grow geometrically. But before I can say anything about the future of American education, or even about the future of American society, a few words are needed about the relationships between schools and their societies in general.

Much of what I have to say here starts quite clearly with the assumption that schools in general, and American schools most particularly, are immensely conservative, status quo-oriented institutions. When it comes to major, society-shaking upheaval, the last place a person would ever want to look for the impetus would be in the schools. After all, their very function—as is the case with law—is conservative: the passing on to a younger generation of an older generation's wisdom and skill. Schools—in any society— are the social system's way of assuring that it will survive, even if that may well be at the expense of some crippled intellects, some stunted creativity, and some broken individual dreams. Whatever their rhetoric might say, schools are, above all, interested in making sure that society—more or less in its present form—continues.

In present-day America, of course, that statement should be repeated and underlined. While there is much present furor over the American schools' teaching of the "basics" (by which is meant reading, writing, and arithmetic), the really basic aspects of America's social system are being perpetuated quite successfully. All of the attitudes, skills, and bits of knowledge appropriate to the members of America's various castes (men, women, blacks, chicanos) and economic classes continue to be distributed appropriately by the schools. They make sure, for example, as a recent Harry Chapin song has it, that the little girls reach for the shelves while the little boys reach for stars. And in what is perhaps the schools' only venture into true egalitarianism, American education makes sure that all of us get a healthy dose of the egalitarian myth: rugged individualism; you can be whatever you want; you get out of it what you put into it.

In such a context (which space simply does not allow me to elaborate here) it would be nothing short of foolhardy to suggest that the American school will lead the way toward major social change. Whatever upheavals we experience during the coming 30 to 50 years—and there are likely to be several—they will not come from the schools. At their best, the schools will try to modify their behavior, belatedly, to catch up with whatever new directions our society takes. At their worst, they will do everything in their power to stand as reactionary guards of values and attitudes that American society is trying to discard.

AMERICAN SOCIETY: TOWARD 2028

If the American school is—at best—a reluctant follower, what kind of society will be dragging it along in the distant year of 2028? I would suggest that there are at least five general aspects of the coming five decades that are sufficiently likely as to be "good bets." Let me summarize these five likelihoods, briefly:

First, the coming 50 years will see a continued presence of problems, shortages, and transitional "bumps" in America's consumption and production of energy. At some point in that 50-year period (and you may pick your own favorite group of "experts" to decide when) the cost (not just in dollars) of petroleum products will get so high that other forms of energy will be mandatory on a large-scale basis. Given our tendency to procrastinate, the chances are good that the transition to other forms of energy will be far from smooth. We will probably not switch until there are enough crises to convince us that we have to. Further, it is not the least bit clear that our choices of alternative energy supplies will be the least bit

wise: judgments made in haste rarely are. The choices in this
area are so fundamental (for example, soft vs. hard technologies,
centralized vs. decentralized energy production, growth vs. steady-
state economy) and so fraught with long-term consequences (especially in the insane, but steady, pursuit of nuclear energy) that I
wouldn't even hazard a guess on how it will all come out 50 years
from now. But it is clear that, for the coming decades, energy will
continue to get more expensive, will continue to be a source of
problems at the national level, and will be the cause of several
localized tragedies (such as shortages in cold winters).

Second, the next 50 years will see an intensification of what
Daniel Bell has referred to as the "service economy." Unlike all
societies in the past, and most in the present, America in the coming 50 years will have the largest (and most rapidly growing) proportion of its workers in the service occupations: health, education,
government, social services, and so forth. The reasons are quite
transparent, being mostly technological: machines can do the work
of people in all other areas of the economy, and we haven't yet figured a way out of our compulsive work ethic, so we have to make or
find jobs elsewhere. Of course, somewhere near the end of the 50-
year span I'm talking about, electronic machines are going to do to
the service sector what mechanical machines did to the production
sector, and then all of our attitudes about work and economics will
really be up against the wall. But, in the meantime, those of us
who work—and most of us will, or will continue to want to—will be
involved in service occupations.

This increase in service occupations, of course, has a direct
two-way impact on education. First, service occupations require
more education than others. This is not, I would argue, because
you have to be smarter or know more to work for governmental
bureaucracies than to work for General Motors, but because the
service occupations have a tradition of respect for credentials, and
you can only get those in schools. Second, educational institutions
are themselves major employers in the service sector. So, the
coming 50 years will see a great deal of the kind of self-serving
that we already see in our schools: education for the sake of sup-
porting educational institutions for the sake of employing more
people.

Third, the major forces that will dictate social change in
America for the coming 50 years will be technological breakthroughs
in two areas: electronics/computers/communications and biomedical/
genetic. Both of these fields are in the midst of what can only be
called a revolution. All forms of electronics are getting faster,
cheaper, smaller, more reliable, and more efficient at a remarkable rate. A new generation of computers that, for all practical

purposes, makes the last one outmoded, is coming along every five years. Home-size computers are already financially accessible to the moderately wealthy (discount stores sell them) and, soon, to people who couldn't dream of buying a home or even a car. Just as the pocket calculator which cost $200 only eight years ago can be outperformed by a new one at $5, so too with the coming generations of computers. This is not to mention equally rapid development in other realms, such as video-cassettes and holography. Again, I would not care to speculate on the impact of these developments— many of which, again, involve important choices between such styles as centralized vs. decentralized—but their continued rapid development is certain. By 2028, for example, it is very likely that I will be able to go to my local discount store and buy a typewriter that I can talk into (in England, a voice-recognition computer can already handle 60 words from any reasonably clear-speaking person), but what that will do to communication in America is far from the realm of wagers I'd care to place.

Similarly, the current developments in genetic and biomedical technology are sure to have profound effects on American society. Birth control that is reliable for both sexes; "test tube" babies (witness the recent birth, again in England, of a child conceived outside the uterus); induced parthenogenesis; genetic engineering; chemical and electrical stimulation of the brain—all will be realities, in one form or another, over the coming 50 years. What that means for a variety of our most cherished institutions (the family, for example) and most deeply entrenched attitudes (such as male chauvinism) is far from certain. But that such developments will proceed, and will—one way or another—form the basis of widespread social change is another sure thing.

Fourth, regardless of what happens in the previously mentioned areas, America will continue to cling to its present modes of stratifying people. Assuming there are no violent revolutions— and they are always possible, though hardly the kind of event I would try to predict—America will continue to provide differential access to wealth and power (and education) depending on a person's sex, race, and social class. While this is hardly the place for an extended discussion of these issues, it should come as no shock to point out that people in power have no great temptation to relinquish their authority. Unless forced to do so, men will retain their substantial privilege over women in America. Whites will continue to oppress people with darker skins. And the rich will guard their wealth and power from the encroachments of the poor. It's not that we rich white males are entitled, biologically or otherwise; it's just that we have so much power, and have so successfully embedded that power in America's institutions (and, I might add, in the minds of Americans, regardless of their caste or class) that it will take a major act of force to take it away from us.

Finally, and again for largely technological reasons, the coming 50 years will see a continued and widespread emergence—not just in America—of something resembling a "Planetary Society." As clichéd as it may sound, the world really is getting smaller and no woman is an island. Technology has a way of spreading that defies national boundaries, and the complexity of international exchange that technology requires can demolish our most comfortable notions of community and "local control." The Arab oil embargo, for example, was able to change the bus schedules of school systems in small western Massachusetts towns in less than a week. Had a group of local, "concerned" citizens attempted to do the same, they would still be setting up committees with no perceptible effect. Whether we like it or not, we are living on a planet that becomes more interdependent every day, and the effects of that mutual dependence will become more powerful and more obvious over the coming decades. There is already, for example, something of a "planetary society" of all those people on the Earth who have, at one time or another, watched Muhammad Ali fight; the impact of television alone over the coming 50 years will be substantial.

Once again, I must bow out when it comes to making any claims about the nature of such an emerging planetary society. Our tendency is to see such developments as wholesome and noble, but I would point out that even the words we use to convey our planetary visions give cause for some alarm: "All men are brothers," we say. Or we urge everyone to recognize "the brotherhood of all men." I guess while we men are bringing the planet together in harmony, the womenfolk will be off in their kitchens cooking our supper! Further, there is a good likelihood that any "Planetary Society" that develops over the coming decades will be a lot more accessible to the rich (and white) than the poor (and not-so-white). But, whatever shape it may take, there can be no doubt that 50 years of forced contact among societies that, very recently, had no awareness of one another at all, will develop some consciousness, among many people, of the fact that we're all in it together.

AMERICAN EDUCATION: TOWARD 2028

These five aspects of America's most likely future will all, of course, have some degree of impact on the schools. I have carefully refrained from making any claims about the nature of those impacts, except in one area (the "service" economy, where the implications are so straightforward as to be obvious). This is largely because the schools' <u>reactions</u> to these developments are not as certain as the developments themselves. For example, as we will see shortly, it is <u>possible</u> that the schools will react to the electronics revolution by jumping in wholeheartedly and adopting a mind-boggling array of new technologies that completely transform the nature of the educational process. But it is at least as likely that the schools will continue to fight, tooth-and-nail, the encroachments of technology of any kind, and that the result of such a battle will be a reluctant implementation of all the worst aspects of centralized electronic wizardry.

There are, however, some features of American education over the next 30 to 50 years that seem to me as likely as the previously mentioned aspects of America's future. First, and perhaps most obvious, is that education in America will extend the range of its clientele. During the coming five decades, formal, institutional education will search out clients from groups that have previously been "out-of-reach." Children will go to public schools at earlier ages, and adults will come back to school to finish degrees, get newly invented ones, or pursue training in skills for new jobs or for "avocations." The notion of "birth-to-death education" will become more and more of a reality. This will largely be due to the economic factors already mentioned, especially in relation to the "service economy." Education will continue to become a larger and larger part of that economy, and clients will have to be drawn from new age groups since the school-age population (ages 5 to 17) will not increase.

Second, the impact of new technologies—particularly in the electronics/communications realm—will be substantial over the next 50 years. While, again, it is not clear whether the schools will welcome or fight these developments, their entry into the school environment in some form is a virtual certainty. Computers, video-tape and video-cassette, microfiche, and even the possible uses of chemical and electrical stimulation of the brain will work their ways, somehow, into the average school. I would even go so far as to suggest—as I have in another context[1]—that the electronic revolution might well, in the next 50 years, make the printed word very close to obsolete. As the price of producing printed matter soars and the price of storing information electronically declines; as more and more people get more and more of their information from nonprinted sources (such as television); and as technological developments make even the everyday uses of the printed word obsolete (witness, for example, the computer-readable markings on consumer items now; or consider the impact of a voice-recognition computer on the need for written job applications), it is more than likely that reading and writing will become unnecessary

for the vast majority of the American population. This is not to
suggest that Americans, in the year 2028, will be more ignorant
and less informed than ever before. Quite the contrary. I would
suggest that 50 years from now we could be the smartest, most
knowledgeable society that has ever existed—and yet be largely illiterate. Whether such a possibility will happen or not is a matter
for sheer speculation, but that the new education-related technologies will find their place in the schools is practically a certainty.

Third, access to education will continue over the next 50
years to be regulated by a person's membership in the right caste
and class. For, of all the institutions which we white, well-off
males have controlled, education is the one on which our hold is
probably the strongest. The relationship between our educational
institutions and the world of work (power and money) is so close
that I see no reason whatsoever to believe that there will be any
shift in the schools' distinct caste/class preferences. Boys will
continue to get educational credentials that stamp them as more
qualified for higher paying, more prestigious, and more powerful
jobs than girls. Whites will continue to receive preferential treatment in all educational institutions. And the rich will continue to
find it easier to get Harvard degrees and Wall Street jobs than the
poor. Until, or unless, America undergoes the kind of major political upheaval that I have already mentioned as a possibility, however remote, the schools will continue to be the servants of those
of us who wield power, and we simply have no interest in using that
power—least of all in the schools—to dethrone ourselves.

Finally, the coming 50 years will see the crude beginnings of
American schools' recognition of the rest of the planet. The growing recognition of our kinship and dependence with all people on
Earth (which I have already mentioned) will force the schools to pay
some attention to cultures, events, and peoples outside our borders.
In fact, as television and other media become more widespread, the
elements of a common global curriculum will already be somewhat
in place, and it will remain for the schools only to adopt them as
their own. I would hesitate, again, to predict with any certainty
what the elements of such a rudimentary universal curriculum might
be, but it seems obvious to me that 50 years from now there will be
some substantial body of knowledge and skill that will be common to
the vast majority of the people on the Earth. Most of that will have
to come about through institutions that are not formally educational
(that is, not tied to the granting of degrees and credentials). The
present-day familiarity of the "Coca-Cola" emblem is an emerging
example. But some of the commonly held values, beliefs, knowledges, and skills that will tie us all to each other in 2028 will have
come from, or at least been reinforced by, our schooling.

As I have already pointed out, this emerging planetary consciousness may not be as rosy as we commonly believe. My guess is that when the schools finally come around to paying attention to the commonality of human experience on Earth, they will end up propagating attitudes and beliefs that are not exactly a solid basis for the full experience of all people's humanity. We frequently talk as if any planet-wide curriculum would do wonders at eliminating the causes of hatred and oppression and even war. But my guess would be that the global curriculum that will evolve over the next several decades will be just as sexist, racist, and elitist as are most of the societies that presently educate their populations in those attitudes separately. In fact, it may well be that one of the forces that will prompt planet-wide curricula will be the growing restlessness of oppressed people everywhere. We who are in power may well join with those in power across the globe to find more effective educational vehicles for keeping ourselves on top. If I were a woman, for example, I would find little comfort in any movement toward planetary consciousness, given the fact that every existing society on the face of the Earth is patriarchal. On a planet where every head-of-state is male, a global curriculum is not very likely to teach females how to reach for the stars.

I have, so far, been talking almost exclusively about what I consider to be the most likely possibilities for the medium-range future. Most of the developments that I have mentioned are sufficiently general to allow a wide range of possibilities within them, and I have repeatedly passed up the opportunity to predict which of those possibilities were most likely. At this point, I would like to plant both feet firmly in the ground of speculation and describe a future for American education that I see as both possible and desirable. I make no claim that there is a high degree of likelihood that American education will go in this direction; in fact, every indication is that this scenario is—at the present time—only a remote possibility. But the educational "system" that I am about to describe is possible by the year 2028 and I present it with the hope that we might find a way to make it a reality.

EDUCATION IN 2028

The following is the script from a television program broadcast on July 17, 2028. Unlike many such broadcasts, this one was for national consumption only, since its subject matter seemed of little concern to people of other nations.

Good evening. As many of you know, today is a momentous occasion for American education, which is why we bring you this

special program on the problems and promise of education in American society. July 17, 2028 seemed an appropriate day for this
broadcast on two important counts: First, it is the twentieth anniversary of the Supreme Court's momentous decision (in the case of
Madloc vs. Massachusetts) ruling compulsory school attendance
laws unconstitutional. Second, today is the day on which the last of
America's former "public schools" was formally closed—a small
elementary school in western Massachusetts. Since we have little
time, it seems inappropriate to mark this anniversary by chron-
icling the history of these past 20 years, as interesting as that
might be to a scholar of American education. Instead, we thought
it more fitting to take a look at the major features of education as
we presently go about it in America, with a special eye toward those
things that seem to be working well as well as those which desper-
ately need improvement. As President Ramirez noted in her in-
augural address, "We have come a long way from the archaic classrooms in which so little learning used to take place. But, however
sophisticated our computerized learning systems might be now,
they have far to go before they provide what we all hope for—a truly
equal opportunity for all Americans to pursue the lives and learnings that suit them best."

If we had to use concise adjectives to describe education in
present-day America, they would certainly include the following:
electronic, decentralized, globally and ecologically aware, and cooperative. But perhaps the most significant thing about the way our
children learn—as compared with the ways in which we of the older
generation were schooled—is the absence of age-segregation, which
was one of the features of the schools derided by that famous Supreme
Court decision. The learning centers that now serve as resources
to all our communities, and the home-used computer programs that
form a basic part of our learning, take no notice of the _age_ of the
"student"—a fact that would have shocked us all as little as 30 years
ago. The mixing of generations in learning at home, on the job, and
in community learning centers has already demonstrated the folly of
our previous ways. After all, it was only three years ago that 16-
year-old Amy Refnal won the Nobel Prize in Physics, and even
Ambou M'tai admits that he could never have produced his world-
acclaimed television movie, "Life-swirl," without the assistance
of his 4- and 5-year-old apprentices.

Let us look first at our accomplishments, for they _are_ impressive. A recent study at the Colad College Institute for Education has shown, for example, that more Americans are knowledgeable in more areas (including literature, the arts, science, mathematics, and current events) than they were in the previous century
(as based on a Harris Poll taken in 1993). This study is particularly

interesting in light of the fact that the researchers also tested the basic literacy of their sample population, and found it to be at an all-time low. No one, I would venture to say, who lived through the "schools" that we of the older generation experienced, could have suspected that it would ever be possible to know so much and read so little. Our home computers and video-discs make the combination of knowledge and illiteracy so easy that we seldom stop to think of how differently people used to look at things.

We can also take pride in the general nature of the <u>content</u> that our learning systems provide for us. Unlike the fragmented subject matter that used to be taught in schools, the subject matter available to us is coherent <u>and</u> diverse. Ever since the International Education Commission began producing its video-computer series on global and ecological issues, there has been widespread availability of high quality instructional materials for anyone who can afford the mere $75 a year that a subscription to their series costs—a very reasonable figure indeed, considering the fact that the home-computer-video-display unit is included at no extra charge. Of course, the programs produced by the American Curriculum Study Committee are also of the highest quality, and I, personally, have seen some of the most stimulating and relevant computer-video series produced and distributed in local communities through their community learning centers.

Compared to the drab, standardized-textbook materials that I had as a school-age child, the content of learning in present-day America is awesome in its variety. Not only do we now employ every conceivable context for learning (except, I would point out, what used to be the standard classroom), but the "subjects" available for study include virtually everything known to personkind. Though it seems ages ago, I can remember clearly the vicious arguments regarding centralization and "Big Brotherism" that occurred when computers began to show promise in homes and schools as educational tools. Had we known then what we know now, those arguments would probably never have taken place. For whatever reasons—perhaps our fear of new technologies in general, and of "invisible" electronics in particular—no one seemed to realize that computers could be programmed to develop their own "software" in a variety of styles once they were fed with appropriate information and wired-in subprograms. Now, of course, it is commonplace for many people to develop very sophisticated computer-video learning programs with no knowledge whatsoever of computer programming or of the electronics of computers—just as, I might add, centuries of authors could write books with no awareness of the technology of printing. The advantage <u>we</u> have over the previous print-oriented societies is that a substantially larger proportion of us are now "authors" and "teachers" than heretofore. While elitism is far from a thing of the past in America, it is nonetheless true that, more and more, people who know something—anything at all—have the capacity to pass that knowledge on to others through their home computers and community learning centers.

Despite these impressive successes, however, American education faces many serious problems. First, and perhaps most important, our attempts to provide equal educational opportunity through the elimination of educational institutions founded on inequity have proved less than adequate. While it is true that all Americans either own or have free access to home computers, community learning centers, and therefore all the educational materials available to anyone else, inequities persist to a rather striking degree. Even with credentialing for professional positions, and for skilled occupations, now based on demonstrated competency and often assessed as fairly as possible through computerized tests, the fact remains that prestigious, powerful, and affluent jobs (and the credentials required to get them) still go disproportionately to the rich, white, and male segments of the population. Many American educators apparently are dumbfounded by this state of affairs, since, on the face of it, our educational system seems so egalitarian. But the fact of the matter is that prejudices against women, nonwhites, and the poor still run high and they continue to be reflected in the learning programs we develop, in the attitudes and values passed on to our children, and in the psychological ease with which people confront various occupational choices. The significant examples of women, minorities, and poor people who have risen to positions of power and prestige to the contrary notwithstanding, we still live in a patriarchal, racist, and class-ridden society, and it remains doubtful that any educational structure could change that. Until a violent revolution happens—if ever—it is extremely doubtful that those who have power in America will voluntarily give up the control they hold so dear.

Second, the American educational system continues to suffer from a badly misguided conception of the need for a basic global curriculum. It has been only ten years since the International Education Commission began broadcasting, via satellites, a basic global curriculum to the myriads of ground stations throughout the world. The curriculum is not, of course, completely acceptable to any particular nation, but it is personkind's first attempt to find those skills, knowledges, attitudes, and values that are sufficiently universal in their usefulness as to be basic to any person's education. There are many of us who find it inexcusable that America is the only major power to refuse to include the Basic Global Curriculum as a part of all educational credentials offered through its computerized degree system. While it is true that Americans can have access to the curriculum whenever they choose, it is one thing to make such a rich and valuable resource available to people, and quite another—considerably more valuable in terms of global survival—to make sure that all people see it as an integral part of their life-long learning.

We do not have sufficient time, in this brief program, to set forth our arguments against the congressional report that refused to make the Basic Global Curriculum a part of all credentialling requirements, but two of their errors in judgment seem blatant enough to deserve attention. First, the Congress's repeated worries over the "lack of sufficient attention to the contributions of Western Civilization" seem to us to entirely miss the point of the curriculum. After all, in a global context, the music of Beethoven deserves no more attention than the equally valid sitar compositions of Shankar or the age-old folk compositions of Nigerian villagers. What the Basic Global Curriculum tries to do is familiarize us with human accomplishments, and we see no reason, other than short-sighted parochialism, for America's increasingly strident claims about the superiority of its particular cultural heritage. Second, the congressional report, instead of offering helpful suggestions for the remaking of the curriculum, seems to take "potshots" at small aspects of it that seem hardly worth such attention. In our opinion, for example, the three-part general structure of the curriculum is soundly conceived, focusing as it does on global, ecological, and technological literacy. In that general context, it seems trivial to argue for 50 pages (as the congressional report does) against the inclusion (in the global literacy section of the curriculum) of a brief segment on the history of patriarchy. Similarly, the report's 37-page attack on the curriculum's single brief mention of unequal distribution of global resources seems to be outright defensiveness, and not in keeping with the overall aim of developing a sound ecological awareness in the Earth's population. It would be refreshing if a political candidate were to emerge who took these issues on straightforwardly as part of her political campaign, so that the International Education Commission could go about the necessary task of revising its curriculum with America's support.

As we close tonight's program, one final word seems necessary, since we have yet to mention what is clearly the most controversial topic these days in American education. We are not prepared to take a firm stand on the issue of cooperation vs. individual competition in education, but we are favorably impressed with the cooperative experiments currently underway, and carefully documented, in Yugoslavia. As the current controversy in America clearly shows, the whole notion of granting occupational credentials,

jobs, and status to working groups rather than to individuals vio-
lates a long tradition of rugged individualism. But it may well be
that America can no longer afford the detrimental effects of individual competition, especially in its educational system. All the
data from Yugoslavia indicate that, when it is clear to people from
the start that they will "pass" or "fail" in their efforts to obtain
educational degrees and credentials only on the basis of the success or failure of the group with which they are associated (in the
Yugoslavian experiments these groups are of ten persons with similar career aims, but Romania is now experimenting with larger
groups of people with mixed career choices and having equally positive results), the results are spectacular—both in terms of individual
accomplishment and in terms of group productivity and cohesiveness.
At the very least, we would urge that similar experiments be undertaken in America, with clear groundrules that guarantee the consti-
tutional rights of the participants.

As we have seen, American education, on this historic day of
the closing of the last American school, has much to be proud of
and much yet to accomplish. We may justifiably be pleased with the
extent to which our present system has made it possible for people
of all ages to learn things of use and meaning to them at any time
in their life. But we must guard carefully against the kind of complacency that could well lead us to overlook the serious deficiencies
in equity and global awareness that our present system perpetuates.

A far-out fantasy, perhaps, but the preceding "scenario" has
many of the elements that seem to me to be crucial to any hopeful
view of America's educational future. I would argue, in fact, that
we have little to look forward to in the year 2028 unless our educational system processes at least the following features:

A major emphasis on global, ecological, and technological
    literacy;

A major reliance on widely accessible media (television,
    radio, home computers linked to larger computers via
    telephone lines, and so on) and a sharply decreased insis-
    tence on reading, writing, and arithmetic as the only ways
    to acquire knowledge;

A destruction of the age-segregation produced by present-day
    schools, which makes it impossible for people of different
    ages to have any idea of each others' lives, much less for
    them to learn anything from each other;

A public, official recognition of the fact that people learn use-
    ful skills and knowledge without the need for professional
    teachers.

It is also worth noting that sexism, racism, and social class are
still alive and well in this scenario. Their elimination in the next
50 years seems so unlikely to me that, however much I would like
to, I can't even remove them from my fantasies of the future.

AND A CHILD SHALL LEAD THEM

For those readers who share at least some of the values I
have espoused above, it seems only fair to begin looking at practical realities. How could American education ever get from where
it presently is to such a bizarre state as I have described? Since
I am clearly not proposing my scenario as a future which is likely
to happen, what kinds of actions would we have to take in the present
to help make it more than just a remote possibility?

The major step, it seems to me, has to do with the way in
which we react, over the next few decades, to the emergence of
the electronic hardware I have been mentioning so frequently. At
the present moment, I would have to admit that the signs are not
exactly auspicious. The vast majority of math teachers, for example, seem to fear the possibility that their students will become
"dependent" on their calculators (strange how we never worry about
people becoming dependent on books). If the general attitude of the
schools, and the general public, toward electronic technologies continues to be hostile, then it is highly unlikely that education will
move in directions which I consider to be desirable. On the other
hand, a mere passive acceptance of whatever technologies come
along will not be so desirable either. After all, the high-technology
industries that are involved in electronics have other motives in
mind than the unselfish promotion of humankind's intellectual capabilities.

What is required over the coming several decades is a positive but humanly aware attitude toward the uses of technology in
education. That, and a lot of hard work to develop the programs
and subprograms that will allow computers, for example, to be
vehicles for people, rather than vice versa. If the only available
instructional materials on television and radio and computer are
those produced by corporate elites, then we will all lose. But if
we find the appropriate ways to mix centralized and decentralized
uses of these technologies, so that anyone can use her home computer to teach something to many other people, then we may well
be on our way to a genuine learning society. Of course, technology
alone, even properly employed, will not achieve a desirable future
for education. We must get started on the development of a basic
global curriculum, even if it is full of errors in judgment and only

succeeds in alienating most nations. For there are, surely, a variety of skills, attitudes, and pieces of knowledge that belong in the "required" learning of all people. We must begin to experiment w'th learning structures that foster cooperation rather than competition, for the schools as they are presently arranged make it virtually impossible for people to use their single most valuable resource—other people. And if we can't find a way to combat the sexism, racism, and classism that seem to be so deeply engrained in our minds and institutions, then we must at least begin to eliminate the absurd degree of age-segregation which the schools play so large a part in. That is a change that the schools could make, and it might well have more far-reaching impact than we think.

As we pursue these seemingly disrelated avenues for restructuring education in America, we will have to be aware of the extent to which what we are doing is political. For schools in general, and the American school in particular, are thoroughly political institutions, by which I mean that they have to do with power, and access to power, in American society. Educators who wish to change the schools and yet disregard the political nature of the educationa' process will, it seems to me, guarantee their own failure. Even those who know that they are playing with political dynamite will find the going more than tough, but they at least have the small advantage of knowing what they're up against and not being put off by battles that they knew they had to fight. To tamper in any meaningful way with the educational process in America (like, I might add, tampering with the family) is to threaten a very sophisticated power structure with a bewildering array of weapons at its disposal. It is no wonder, and no mere accident, that the turbulent 1960s gave way to the flaccid 1970s.

If there is any hope for the kind of sweeping reform of American education that I am proposing, it resides in the minds and hearts of the system's victims—children. It is already clear that children learn far more outside of school than they do within its walls. In fact, they learn more from television alone than they do in school, and that despite the abominable nature of commercial television. I am not sure that, when seen in this way, it is exactly a fair fight—the naive children of America vs. a power structure that has succeeded in molding all previous generations to its own purposes—but children are possessed of remarkable and ever-surprising resources.

My almost-five-year-old son, Adam, informed me the other day that he doesn't think he'll always believe what his teachers say in kindergarten. "If they tell me I did something dumb," he said, "I'll just figure they were wrong and it won't bother me." I can't even describe how much I hope he's right about that, and if he is right there's at least a chance that schooling will be dead, and learning alive, in the year 2028.

NOTE

1. "Illiterates with Doctorates: The Future of Education in an Electronic Age," The Futurist, August 1978, pp. 243-44.

ABOUT THE EDITOR
AND CONTRIBUTORS

PETER H. WAGSCHAL is an Associate Professor and the Director of the Future Studies Program in the School of Education at the University of Massachusetts. Wagschal has published numerous articles on education and Futurism in such journals as The Futurist and Phi Delta Kappan. He is currently editing a collection of R. Buckminster Fuller's essays on education, to be published by the University of Massachusetts Press in fall 1979.

R. BUCKMINSTER FULLER, the keynote speaker at "Learning Tomorrows," is an internationally acclaimed poet, philosopher, architect, and mathematician. He holds 40 honorary degrees in ten different disciplines. Fuller's magnum opus, Synergetics, describes the philosophy behind his best-known inventions, including the geodesic dome and the "dymaxion-sky-ocean-world" map.

WILMA SCOTT HEIDE is former Board Chairone and then President of NOW, National Organization for Women, Inc., the world's largest feminist organization. Heide is a speaker and writer, both in the United States and internationally, a consultant to other educators and leaders, and a former Human Rights Commissioner.

IVAN ILLICH is the former Vice-Rector of the Catholic University of Puerto Rico and Director of the Center for Intercultural Documentation in Cuernavaca, Mexico. Illich is the author of Deschooling Society, Tools for Conviviality, and Medical Nemesis, among others, and has been a leading figure in radical educational thought.

GREGORY ANRIG is the Commissioner of Education for the Commonwealth of Massachusetts.

JONATHAN KOZOL is a teacher, writer, and critic. Author of Death at an Early Age, The Night Is Dark and I Am Far from Home, and Children of the Revolution, Kozol is a major spokesman for the Free Schools movement. He is presently working on a book regarding desegregation in the Boston Public Schools.

163

HENRI DIEUZEIDE is Director of the Division of Structures, Content, Methods and Techniques of Education of UNESCO in Paris, France. Mr. Dieuzeide is a former Director of Public Television in France, and attended "Learning Tomorrows" as a representative of the Director General of UNESCO, Mr. M'Bow.

ELISE BOULDING is a futurist, feminist, and sociologist currently serving as a professor at the University of Colorado. Boulding has published extensively on women's roles in society, peace education, and world order issues. Her most recent book is The Underside of History: A View of Women Through Time.

MARIO FANTINI is the Dean of the School of Education at the University of Massachusetts, a leader of the Alternative Schools Movement, and the author of numerous books on education. Fantini's most recent work, Alternative Education, is considered to be the leading source book in the field.

HAZEL HENDERSON is a futurist and activist, and author of Creating Alternative Futures: The End of Economics. She is also a member of the Advisory Council of the United States Congress Office of Technology Assessment.

DWIGHT W. ALLEN is University Professor of Urban Education at Old Dominion University. He is the former Dean of the School of Education at the University of Massachusetts. Allen is a leading spokesman for educational innovation, and the originator of modular scheduling, differentiated staffing, and microteaching.